WILLKIE SPRINT

Photo courtesy of Indiana University Archives.

WILLKIE SPRINT

A STORY OF FRIENDSHIP, LOVE, AND WINNING
THE FIRST WOMEN'S LITTLE 500 RACE

KERRY HELLMUTH

INDIANA UNIVERSITY PRESS

This book is a publication of

Indiana University Press
Office of Scholarly Publishing
Herman B Wells Library 350
1320 East 10th Street
Bloomington, Indiana 47405 USA

iupress.org

Manufactured in the United States of America

First printing 2024

Cataloging information is available from Library of Congress.

978-0-253-06985-6 (hardback)
978-0-253-06986-3 (paperback)
978-0-253-06987-0 (ebook)

To Mom and Dad,
who give so readily and whose words and actions
still serve as my guide

To Gino and Giorgio,
my everything,
with whom I love swapping stories

CONTENTS

BEFORE I START

ALL OUR STORIES ARE BUILT on the foundation laid by those who came before us. With respect to the inaugural Little 500 for women, I was able to thank some—such as the members of the Kappa Alpha Theta team (often referred to herein as simply the Thetas), Spero Pulos, and Phyllis Klotman—in person because they were there when the race came to fruition. Others came long before I arrived on campus or even before I was born, and I have given credit to just a few of them within these pages. I know there are thousands more. So many others were important to *my* story, from my family to Rob-Bob to my roommate Karen and other dorm mates to my Willkie Sprint teammates and co-riders from other teams to my professors and classmates. Thank you all for contributing to these happenings in 1988—it was one heck of a start to my adult life!

Thirty-five years have passed between the events in this book and my taking the time to write them down. This story tells what I lived through during my freshman year of college at Indiana University. I present the events and my family, friends, boyfriend, professors, and others according to my memory but also according to what I know or knew of the people involved. I sought to be accurate in recounting the gist of the events, but some may not be retold exactly as they actually happened. I am getting to the age where I might not remember what someone told me yesterday, much less years ago. To facilitate this story, I have taken liberties in re-creating conversations and even minor events from 1987 and 1988. While many details of those years remain crystal clear in my memory, I cannot profess to recall every detail with accuracy. I used my imagination and knowledge of the people involved to fill in a few blanks. Also, since I only truly know my own perspective, I focus this story on my life and my team. Well over 130 female students participated in the inaugural year of the women's Little 500 race, but I mention only a few of the riders from other teams due to space constraints. At the request of some members of the 1988 Kappa Alpha Theta team, all the personal names of that team's members and coaches have been removed from this story—certainly no indication that I do not hold the highest respect for them and their contributions to the creation of the women's Little 500. Each student involved had her own unique experience of the year we spent together riding around the oval track at Bill Armstrong Stadium. I imagine that most were as spectacular as my own, the only story I feel qualified to tell.

WILLKIE SPRINT

PROLOGUE

I HAD NOT THOUGHT ABOUT the Little 500 bicycle race in years when the following showed up in my inbox.

Hi Kerry,

I hope this email finds you well. I'm working on a potential story focused on the first women's Little 500 race. If you have some time, I'd love to connect via phone or Zoom. Happy to work around your schedule.

Thank you and hope to hear from you soon!

Best, *Austin Francalancia*

The first thing I did was google this Austin chap. Who was he, was he legit, how did he get my email address? What I discovered was that he was a film producer who had worked on *The Dark Knight Rises*, *Borat Subsequent Moviefilm*, *Chef*, *The Mars Generation*, and a host of other film and TV productions. He had won an Emmy. He was definitely legit.

My curiosity satisfied—and piqued, actually—I agreed to chat with Austin via Zoom. We arranged a time that took into account the seven-hour difference between our time zones, mine in Italy and his in the US. In the end, I pushed it back an hour so I could fit in a bike ride and met up with him on Zoom just out of the shower with wet hair. Somehow it was fitting that I managed to fit in my ride before talking about the year that had given birth to my lifelong passion for riding a bicycle, in any form, anywhere.

It turns out that Austin was also a graduate of Indiana University. Given the devastating effects of COVID-19 on the film industry, Austin had actually just moved from LA back to his home state of Indiana with his wife and fifteen-month-old son. I recalled the quiet and charm of the neighborhoods in Bloomington, Indiana, where I had spent my days as an undergraduate. With its beautiful tree-lined streets and its laid-back vibe, Bloomington harkened back to the fifties in some ways. No one seemed to be in a hurry. There was rarely traffic. The university's quietly majestic limestone buildings with red roofs, sprawling lawns, and wooded areas really made it feel that student life was the heart of the small city. Austin and his family were probably happy to have settled in the peaceful college town.

But to the point: Austin wanted to focus a feature film on the collegiate bicycle race that my team and I had won over thirty years earlier. Little 500 had defined my entire college experience, not just that first year when my team and I won the historic inaugural women's race. Austin and I chatted about the race, and he told me that he had met with Phyllis Klotman's family members.

The image of Dean Phyllis Klotman rose in my mind. She was small in stature but had a firecracker of a personality. Growing up as an Orthodox Jew in a poor family, she suffered discrimination of all sorts. She related to the struggle of African Americans and focused her academic career on bringing light and recognition to their lives. As a professor of African American studies and film studies, Klotman established IU's Black Film Center & Archive and worked tirelessly to preserve and celebrate authentic minority stories.

Tiny but capable and tough, Phyllis Klotman was a natural choice to serve as the dean for women's affairs at a large university, a role requiring leadership through difficult transitions within the traditional academic setting. Klotman was up for the job. Legend has it that IU basketball coach Bobby Knight—a towering and famously intimidating figure at six feet five inches—had once knelt before her and begged her to release several players from academic probation so they could play in the NCAA tournament.

Back in 1987, I was enjoying my senior year at West High School in Madison, Wisconsin. But down in Bloomington, Indiana, Dean Klotman was following the trials and tribulations of the Kappa Alpha Theta sorority's bicycle team and possible history being made. The entirely female Theta team was attempting to qualify for the Little 500 bicycle race—against teams consisting of only male students. They were not the first women who had tried to qualify for the Little 500 race, but the Theta team had garnered a lot of media attention and support around campus. On the spring day they made their qualification attempt, the stands of the IU Little 500 track were predominated by fans cheering for them.

Never heard of the Little 500? Let me catch you up. The Little 500 at Indiana University is the country's largest collegiate bicycle race and supports scholarships for working students. Riders compete in four-person relay teams racing their bicycles around a quarter-mile cinder track. Modeled on the Indianapolis 500 car race, the Little 500 started in 1951 and quickly became an annual tradition, pitting fraternity and dormitory teams against each other. Throngs of fans—friends, family, classmates, and Bloomington citizens—show up to support the teams, and their loud cheering can be heard all across campus.

Children of the seventies and eighties have heard of the Little 500. In 1979, the race gained notoriety as the subject of the Academy Award–winning film *Breaking Away* and a short-lived TV series that spun off from the movie. The actual race has been covered by national media and television, including major networks such as ESPN. It offers a collegiate spectacle that garners a huge crowd watching the race live and, I would guess, a sizable TV-viewing public. Television viewers are treated to some worthwhile entertainment, particularly thrilling to those of us who attended IU or even raced in "Little 5." We are transported back to the good old days at Bill Armstrong Stadium.

Years earlier, the Little 500 race had been dreamt up by Howdy Wilcox Jr., the president of the IU Foundation. Legend has it that Howdy was strolling through campus one crisp fall afternoon in 1950 and witnessed an informal bicycle race. Students leaned out of dorm windows, yelling out support for their classmates who raced their bicycles around the building.

The scene and the students' raucous support of the racers started Howdy thinking. His father, Howdy Sr., had won the Indy 500 car race. Wanting to involve students in the mission of the IU Foundation, Howdy Jr. had suggested to IU's then-president Herman B Wells the idea of a student council to promote the foundation. On campus that day, observing the camaraderie of the students racing their bikes and cheering each other on gave Howdy the spark that led to the creation of the Little 500 bicycle race. He met with President Wells and started planning a competitive bicycle race for the students. Why not tie in the creation of a miniature foundation run by the students themselves? The money raised by charging for admission tickets could be used to fund scholarships for working students.

The Little 500 race and the Indiana University Student Foundation (IUSF) were born. As for the race, Howdy modeled it on the Indy 500 car race that had meant so much to his father. The students would race around a cinder track for a total of two hundred laps just like the race car drivers, the students riding fifty miles to the drivers' five hundred. Competitors had to qualify for the race, and the winner had the "pole position." Racers would line up in a three-by-eleven starting grid just as the Indy 500 drivers did. Each team had a pit where the team members and mechanic could be present on the track.

The bicycle race would mimic the grand pageantry and spectacle of the Indy 500 car race as well. Howdy drew on his connections to the famous car race and brought both the official Indy 500 announcer and its chief steward to Bloomington. The cyclists started the race with a pace lap following a pace car driven by Wilbur Shaw, three-time winner of the Indianapolis 500 and president of the Indianapolis Motor Speedway. IU President Wells was in the passenger seat.

So it was that in 1951, the inaugural Little 500 race was attended by seven thousand spectators cheering on the cyclists, a huge success by any measure. It foreshadowed the remarkable success that the event has enjoyed ever since. Within a few years, events and parties were added to round out the weekend. The Little 500 bicycle race became the star and central attraction of the "World's Greatest College Weekend." Eventually Howdy Wilcox Jr. took over the job of waving the finish line's checkered flag himself.

Only male students participated in the Little 500 at its inception in 1951. No rule in the official rulebook, the "Little 500 Race Bible," prevented women from racing. The participation of female students at first involved support activities, such as sewing banners to hang around the stadium and in the pits. There was, however, a short-lived tradition between two Greek sorority houses: from 1951 to 1960, the Delta Gamma women competed against the Kappa Alpha Theta women in an event called the Little Little 500. In a relay race around an oval, each team member had to carry an egg on a spoon and keep it upright while exchanging both their bicycle and the egg. The number of points obtained by completing the race fastest and dropping the egg the least number of times determined the winner of the fitting prize, an eggbeater.[1]

The women were thrown a bone in 1955 when a contributing event was added to round out the Little 500 race weekend. It was the first running of the Mini 500, in which female students competed on large tricycles. Yes, *trikes*, larger versions of the children's toy. It is hard to fathom today because it seems absurd and incredibly sexist to relegate the women to a few laps looking like overgrown children riding on toys while the men were able to compete in a full-on fifty-mile cycling relay. No more sexist than women riding around balancing eggs on spoons, mind you. I suppose the idea of a tricycle race was considered an improvement. Remember that it was the 1950s, long before feminism truly took hold.

As it turns out, riding bicycles has held an important and pivotal role throughout the evolution of feminism. In the 1850s, the revolutionary shift from wearing skirts to bloomers, loose trousers tapered at the knee to allow more freedom of movement, was named for one particularly spirited advocate of women's rights, Amelia Bloomer.

I knew of her because my mom and dad had a running joke about Bloomer and bloomers. My parents met while Mom was in college and Dad in law school at Marquette University. My mom and her college girlfriends were navigating an evolving territory. It was 1960, and young women were caught between toeing the line of our gendered past and dreaming of what feminism offered. One Christmas, trying to demonstrate both his devotion to my mom and his support for feminism, my dad gave her a book about Amelia Bloomer. Mom could not hide her disappointment in the gift. It was not that she had anything against Bloomer or women's rights. Probably she simply hoped for a beautiful wool sweater to keep her warm during the cold Wisconsin winter or any one of about one hundred other more personal gifts rather than that book. Anyway, it became a running joke between the two of them.

Back in her day, Amelia Bloomer had famously taken to bicycling in her version of a split skirt, the only way to navigate the first bicycles. Bloomers led the way in a clothing reform that was essentially fueled by women's growing interest in gaining freedom and independence—on a bike. Amelia, her bloomers, and the idea of women riding bicycles were criticized as a dangerous promotion of female immodesty. Amelia and her cronies sought emancipation from the restrictive petticoats representing their repression. There were those who opposed the idea—those who thought women should not ride bikes. In addition to preventing the ability to ride a bicycle, it turns out that petticoats and layers of skirts were actually a fire hazard for the women wearing them. The stiff crinoline bearing the steel under-hoops of women's petticoats was flammable. Women were "literally trapped . . . in a large cage that was difficult to escape from and covered in flammable fabric at a time when open flame was common."[2] Escaping this dress would allow women the ability not only to move more freely and actively but also, and maybe more importantly, not to catch on fire, a fate which apparently killed thousands of women.[3]

Over the ensuing decades, the use of bloomers was increasingly adopted by women wishing to gain independence of movement. The Rational Dress Society was born in 1881 and protested, God bless them, against clothing deforming the body or impeding movement. More specifically, they implicated the corset, high-heeled shoes, heavily weighted skirts, and the multiple layers of crinolines and underwear. The society suggested that women should wear no more than seven pounds of underwear, a bold statement in an era when typically they wore *twice* that amount.[4] You can't make these facts up!

As bicycles developed from the penny-farthing style to the modern bicycle, even more women began riding them. Finally giving women their own convenient modes of transport, bicycles freed women from restrictive lifestyles and wardrobes—and from fourteen pounds of highly flammable underwear! I definitely have Amelia and her supporters to thank—and not only because I am not a big fan of skirts. Frankly, there is not much that I love more than riding a bicycle.

Until I took Women and Literature L207 in my first semester as a freshman at Indiana University, I had never really felt much connection with women of Amelia Bloomer's era. Watching films depicting women of that period, those wearing fourteen pounds of undergarments including tightly fitted corsets and layers of crinolines and petticoats, I had always marveled at the elaborate dress of the day. Those skirts! With how long I figured it took them to get dressed, I was thankful that times had changed and I was not required to dress that way. But I had not connected the dots. Clothing had not evolved without a fight. It had escaped me that bold actions on the part of Amelia Bloomer, the suffragists, and the women of the Rational Dress Society had been crucial to changing how women dressed.

Women and Literature was taught by a leading scholar, Professor Susan Gubar. I knew she was a superstar when I picked up the book for class. *The Norton Anthology on Women in Literature* was a thick, cream-colored book, boasting nearly twenty-five hundred tissue-paper-thin pages within its hard cover. Gubar's name was boldly emblazoned on the cover as a coeditor.

Throughout our initial lessons, the light of the afternoon sun shone into our classroom and cast dancing shadows as it filtered through the leaves of the tall oak trees surrounding Ballantine Hall. As autumn progressed, our eyes were drawn outside the window to the branches boasting spectacular shades of orange and yellow. Our eyes maybe, but not our attention. Our attention stayed fixed on Susan Gubar. Eventually the colors faded and leaves fell away. We did not mind, because we had become more and more enraptured by her literary criticism and analysis. As the end of the semester neared, the progressively longer shadows yielded to no sunshine at all, as we marched toward the winter solstice. By that point, we were too entranced to even notice.

"'There's nothing on earth so savage—except a bear robbed of her cubs—as a hungry husband.'" We giggled, and Professor Gubar continued. "What, *what exactly*, do you think the people of her day thought when Fanny Fern published those words? What was the reason her columns earned her more than any other columnist of her day?" she asked us in her New York accent, adding as she stepped forward for emphasis, "*Any* columnist, male *or* female?" She went on, shaking her head back and forth before popping her reading glasses out of her curly brown hair, "How exactly did Fanny Fern achieve being the *highest* paid columnist in 1853 when writing lines like this: 'O, girls! set your affections on cats, poodles, parrots or lap-dogs; but let matrimony alone. It's the hardest way on earth of getting a living'?"

Reaching far beyond the typical masters of Austen, the Brontë sisters, and Dickinson, we delved into the rich offerings of the anthology—the works of Mary Wollstonecraft, Phillis Wheatley, Fanny Fern, and so many others. The writings of these important authors were inextricably linked to the condition of women in their respective eras. Prof. Gubar presented my class with famous literary works that brought to life the long struggle for equality that we women had apparently endured.

It was a battle I did not know much about. Sure, I had heard about it. Feminism and all that. My mom was about as proud a feminist as existed. But I really had not experienced much gender discrimination in my own life. Mom was particularly ardent in assuring her daughters from day one that they were capable of doing anything boys could do. I did not doubt her. I confidently followed my brothers in pursuing any type of adventure or sport. In the end, I joined far more sports teams than they ever did. And if I did not have soccer or swim practice after school, I played hours of touch football with the neighborhood kids (boys). In my family, the chores, such as washing dishes after dinner or setting and clearing the table, were shared equally among my brothers, sisters, and me on a rotating basis. We each had the equal opportunity to earn a crisp one-dollar bill if we went to three swim practices per week. We were treated equally. There was no differentiation based on sex.

Professor Gubar's course provided me with rich and aching portraits of why feminism was so important. It had not always been this way. I learned that audacious Mary Wollstonecraft had to take up her precious time making the elaborate argument that women were not inferior to men. (It was just their lack of education, she argued.)

At first, I was not so sure I liked Professor Gubar's class. Some of the literature made me uncomfortable. I felt sadness and anger when learning about the injustices women faced. There was something else too: I understood that *feminism* was perceived by some as a dirty word. Facing down the truths of our collective past, I knew that I was, we all were, indebted to those who fought for our equal rights. But I somehow wanted to lay claim to those rights without the vestige of that controversial F-word (feminism) and the bra-burning association that it had carried forth since the 1960s. I wanted to be a feminist. But I also wanted to be cool. Susan Gubar was clearly both. If true education is the opening of minds, Prof. Gubar was a master. We were treated to eloquent literary voices but also forced to sit in the discomfort of past inequality. And so we grew. I had to decide where I stood. We all did.

We did not read anything by Amelia Bloomer, but we might have. She was a women's rights activist and writer too. I want to see her as simply a woman who rejected bulky clothing in favor of split skirts and bloomers because she wanted to ride a bike. But history teaches that these women had to buck societal expectations. They had to face scorn and rejection. Their courage was driven by the joy of riding a bicycle and the freedom it offered. Not only riding for pleasure's sake, but also as a mode of transportation. Bicycles offered independence. Why was the world back then so scared of giving women independence? Their simple desire for joy and freedom was seen as radical. It is barely perceivable to me, or anyone born in today's world, how anyone could classify the desire to ride a bicycle as so radical. History sucks, as someone else has surely said. I, in turn, say this: Thank you to Mary Wollstonecraft, to Amelia Bloomer, and to the other women who hopped on the bike and took up the pen.

Back in the 1960s and '70s, I am pretty sure that the women riding tricycles around in circles in Indiana University's Assembly Hall did not experience the same sense of euphoria as Amelia Bloomer. But they certainly had fun. Oftentimes dressed in comical costumes, they provided a wholesome side-show during the Little 500 weekend. The Mini 500 attracted huge crowds of over five thousand students from its early years onward, and the riders seemingly had a blast training and racing on those overgrown trikes. The Mini provided an outlet for the women. Consistently drawing large crowds, the Mini 500 looked so fun that by 1977, male students were even allowed to take part in the trike race. The difference was that the male students were able to *choose* whether to race trikes or bikes. Let's face it: that's a big difference.

After the Little 500 race was memorialized by Hollywood, even more IU students with athletic ability dreamed of riding in it. In 1979, the Little 500 race attained legendary status due to the release of the movie *Breaking Away*. The film's fictional story centered on a group of "townies" competing against the fraternities in the Little 500 race. The film was nominated for five Academy Awards, including Best Picture, as well as four Golden Globe awards. Its screenwriter, Steve Tesich, had grown up in Bloomington and attended IU, where he had been an alternate rider for his fraternity's Little 500 team. He wrote what he knew—the screenplay was based on his own experiences and those of another racer of his time. Tesich's homegrown story won the highest accolades, both the coveted Oscar for Best Original Screenplay and the highest Golden Globe award, for Best Film. Waving the checkered flag as the townie Cutters team won the race, Howdy Wilcox Jr. played himself in the film.

With the growing popularity and national notoriety of the Little 500 race, female students became more and more interested in joining their male counterparts at the track. Fun aside, the Mini 500 race offered little satisfaction for female athletes interested in riding a *bicycle* in the Little 500.

In 1973, the first team consisting of all women requested entry into the Little 500 race. After initially denying their request, the IUSF reversed their position following the filing of a complaint with the Bloomington Human

Rights Commission by the six women.[5] It was determined that the women could take part in the race. All they had to do was qualify.

So began the numerous attempts by teams consisting partially or entirely of women. In each of the earliest attempts in the 1970s and early '80s, the teams including women failed to make the cut at the Little 500 Qualifications race. (In the case of the 1973 team, they won the appeal based on human rights but then were unable to compete due to another rule, which precluded transfer students.) Lacking a race of their own, the only route for women's teams was trying to enter the men's race. The catch was that the race day format was limited to inclusion of the fastest thirty-three teams, as determined by the official Qualifications race, and there were often over fifty teams trying to make the cut. "Quals" was a fun day at the track every year. Random draw determined the start time for each team's qualifying attempt. Each team had three attempts possible to log their fastest four-lap qualifying time.

How does a team perform the qualification attempt to earn a spot in the Little 500 race? Using a flying start, a qualification attempt consists of four teammates racing one lap each. They must exchange the bicycle with one another between each lap, and that hand-off must occur within the thirty-two-foot exchange zone. The fastest thirty-three teams to complete the four laps with bicycle exchanges qualify for the race, thus determining the official starting grid for the Little 500 race. Those unfortunate teams clocking a slower time than the thirty-third team, after months of planning and training, have their dream of riding in the Little 500 shattered in roughly three minutes' time. The first all-female team to ride in Qualifications, Team Double Take, had tried and failed to qualify in 1981.

Would the women of the Kappa Alpha Theta sorority who were trying to qualify for the 1987 Little 500 race have better results? The Thetas dropped the bike during their first attempt and were placed at the end of the qualifying teams. They messed up an exchange on their second attempt. Limited to three attempts each, teams that had a qualifying time that was too slow—i.e., not within the top thirty-three teams' times—were repositioned at the end of the group. After all teams had made a first attempt, those wishing could make a second qualifying attempt. And then, later in the day, even a third attempt.

The Thetas had some fans there for their first attempt. Being a sorority making a historical attempt to enter the men's Little 500 race was obviously quite a big deal and an honor, so their Theta sisters showed up to cheer them on. But their fans were not limited to the sorority membership. As the day progressed, more and more students and fans appeared. Even those who had come to cheer on other teams were inevitably drawn to the cause of the four determined Theta women trying to make history. They were a crowd favorite. Everyone loves an underdog.

People watching could see that they were close, that quite possibly they were going to ride their way into history by becoming the first ever women's team to qualify for the Little 500. If only they could nail their exchanges. There was a lot of press that day, including a radio announcement about the sorority team trying to make history.

The Thetas had a gap between their second attempt and what would be their third and final qualification attempt, and they returned to their sorority. The young assistant director of the IUSF, Spero Pulos, hopped in his car, left Quals, and drove to their sorority to offer encouragement. These coeds simply wanted the chance to race their bikes in the Little 500 race like their male counterparts could, and he wanted to offer support.

The Kappa Alpha Theta sorority team was made up of strong athletes. They had poured all of their physical prowess into preparing to qualify for the Little 500 race. Upon their return to the track for their third attempt, a large fleet of Theta sorority sisters were present and yelling their lungs out in support. But not only their sisters were cheering. The number of people watching had grown quite a bit. Everyone present was on their feet cheering for the Thetas' qualification effort. It had been clear from their first attempt that the Thetas were on the bubble to secure a spot in the race, so fans provided loud moral support.

Finally they took the track for the third time that day. A rousing and collective round of applause rose from the stands as the Thetas' final rider sprinted in to clinch a time qualifying well above thirty-third place. They had done it! They had logged four laps in 3:03.72, a time that qualified them for the Little 500 race. So far.

Other teams had also botched earlier exchanges. Like the Thetas, these teams were allowed subsequent attempts to qualify for the race. Several of these teams were able to beat the Thetas' qualifying time. Their time did not hold, and the later teams bumped the Thetas out of the thirty-third spot and effectively out of the Little 500 race.

However, a women's edition became undeniable. The qualification attempt by the Kappa Alpha Theta sorority sisters finally tipped the scales toward change. Two other all-female teams, named Stonies and Spokeswomen, had also participated in some Little 500 Series events that year, as had a handful of other female students. The female riders, whose collective results begged the question of a women's Little 500 race, already had the support of Spero and the IUSF. It was high time the university acknowledged their keen interest in competing as well. Fortunately, they gained the interest and support of Dean Klotman. With her highly developed radar for injustice, she had started following the plight of the female riders closely that Little 500 season. It was decided over the summer that a women's race would be offered. From the efforts of these female riders and the support of both the IUSF and the academic dean, the women's Little 500 race was finally born. In the following year, female students would finally have a chance to compete in a race of their own—not one requiring them to balance an egg on a spoon and not in a tricycle race. Female students would be racing around the oval at Bill Armstrong Stadium on two wheels.

Lucky me. Oblivious to the battle of the Thetas and so many other female riders before them, I was to arrive the following year as a freshman. Oblivious to the gruesome history of women burning alive in crinoline fires, I was to don some cycling shorts and hop on a Roadmaster bicycle. Oblivious to the absurdity of grown women being offered a tricycle race, I was to participate in the long-fought-for first edition of the women's Little 500. This is my story.

CHAPTER

CHOOSING THE UNIVERSITY or college where you will pass four years of life can be daunting. Expensive schools were not really an option in our family with five kids, but I doubt that they would have interested me much anyway. As it turned out, my friend Roxanne invited me on a long driving trip to visit her schools of interest during the summer before our senior year of high school. I headed off for the two-week road trip with Roxanne, her parents, and two German teenage exchange students they were hosting for the summer, Nico and Daniela. Roxy's parents had set up appointments to tour the campuses at universities including Duke, University of North Carolina, William and Mary, University of Virginia, Clemson, and Vanderbilt. The trip was a blast—four teenagers in the back of an Econoline van playing cards and swapping mixtapes with one another to play on our Sony Walkmans. The highlight was five nights spent at a Hilton Head hotel right on the beach. But neither Roxy nor I came home inspired by the universities we visited.

They were, of course, her choices—or maybe even the colleges her parents chose for her—and not mine. I knew that the schools were out of reach for me without sizable student loans, but I tried to give them a fair look. I am sure my parents breathed a sigh of relief when I reported that none of the schools on our trip appealed to me.

To round out our search, my mom took Roxy and me to see a few schools in the Big Ten Conference, large public institutions established by state land grants. Northwestern was too urban, we decided in unison. University of Illinois at Urbana-Champaign boasted a pretty campus, but I knew somehow—maybe just a feeling but one I trusted—that it was not for me. Marching around campus on a gray day with an engineering student as our guide, we agreed that Purdue held little appeal. At Indiana University, we both knew nearly upon exiting the car: we had (both) found our spot. The enclosed campus boasted all the manicured beauty of the eastern schools we had visited, but Bloomington had a far more relaxed midwestern vibe. Any pretension we had noted elsewhere certainly did not exist in the sleepy south central Indiana college town.

On a sunny fall day, the IU campus is hard to beat. Its stunning canopy boasts over twenty species, including yellowwood, sugar maple, flowering dogwood, tulip, and ginkgo trees. Well-maintained gardens and amazing flower beds cap off the natural beauty, and the man-made structures are no less impressive. The university buildings were crafted using the same stately Indiana limestone used to construct the Empire State Building. Quarried right there in central Indiana, the classic limestone complemented the campus's Gothic and art deco architectural styles well. I felt an immediate connection to the place. In the end, Roxanne applied to a number of schools. I applied to just one. With decent SAT scores and high school grades, I was admitted early, and that was that.

In August 1987, just a few days after my eighteenth birthday, my dad and I packed up the family VW Rabbit and made the journey from my own college town home of Madison, Wisconsin, down to Bloomington. The loaded moment, the one that every parent dreads and every young high school graduate looks forward to, had arrived: the college drop-off. At some point during our seven-hour drive, I remember Dad recounting to me the story of the moment that he had dropped my brother Dave off at University of Minnesota three years earlier. Apparently Dave had opened the car door outside of his dorm upon arrival, spread his arms wide, and said loudly, "Finally!" I made a point not to do the same.

Feeling ready and excited to start college life, I settled into my room on the top (eleventh) floor of Willkie North, an all-female tower that was paired with the all-male Willkie South. A dining hall between the two completed the complex; there, I ended up getting a part-time job where several months later I served peaches to a cute boy living in Willkie South. He became my first love, but we will get to that in time.

I felt relieved and fortunate when I met my roommate, Karen. I remember the apprehension before she arrived and during those months before I headed off to college. I wondered if we would get along well and hoped that we would. Any fears dissipated upon meeting her. An out-of-state student like me, hailing from Cincinnati, Ohio, Karen arrived with a big smile and lots of energy. She was fun-loving, and we became fast friends. We were a good match—both being out-of-state and academically motivated students. A big bonus was that her father was skilled at constructing anything we needed for our little space. He took measurements of the beds and showed up a few weeks later with a perfectly measured loft for my bed that gave us way more space.

In our outward appearances, Karen and I were opposites. While I was tall and dark, Karen was short, blond, and freckled. But we gelled right away, chatting, laughing, blasting music, and belting out the words to songs like the Cure's "Close to Me" and Prince's "When Doves Cry" as we decorated our living space, bought our supplies at the college bookstore, and ate late-night pizza. As we checked out campus and downtown, we joked that Karen took two steps for every one of mine, her little legs motoring along. While she measured less than five feet tall, Karen nonetheless matched my quick pace with ease. Together, Karen and I bemoaned the fact that, on our long V-shaped dormitory floor, we had been unlucky enough to land the corner room directly across from Crystal, the senior student RA whose job it was to supervise our entire floor.

At the welcome meeting for the students on our floor, Crystal told us that the dorm wanted to enter a team in the women's Little 500 bicycle race. My hand shot up when she asked who was interested in riding in the race. A tomboy who had always tried to keep up with two older brothers, I had competed in every sport that came my way growing up. My childhood neighborhood was filled with big families, and we kids were outside playing endlessly. Soccer and football in the street. Hours spent trying to perfect riding a wheelie (I never did). Winters full of pickup hockey games at the local park. Endless rounds of basketball and H-O-R-S-E in Katie McCormick's driveway court. I did even more of the same on teams. Starting at age five with both swim team and soccer team, over the following years I also joined T-ball, softball, tennis, volleyball, and basketball teams, followed by running cross-country and doing triathlons in high school. Needless to say, I committed to racing in the first women's Little 500 bicycle race for my dormitory team in an instant upon hearing about it.

Soon enough, signs appeared all over our dorm: "Love to ride a bike? Join our Little 500 team! Come learn more." I planned to attend the informational meeting that would take place a few weeks later. I tried to talk Karen into joining me. Following the lead of the organizers who clearly understood the never-ending hunger of eighteen-year-olds, I pointed to the promise of free pizza to all who attended. Karen was unpersuaded. In fact, she looked at me as if I were crazy. Either crazy for suggesting she do the race or crazy for wanting to participate myself, I was not sure which. I got the same response from my other new college dormitory friends. It seemed that there were not too many high school athletes like myself. Those who *had* participated in high school sports seemed happy to have replaced them with the oh-so-satisfying college activities of (a) partying and (b) excessive lounging.

This revealed what I had started to perceive from my first days on campus: I was a fish out of water. There were not many matches for my athletic sensibility and love of competing in any sport, any time. As far as my effort to convince Karen went, I failed. However, to her credit—at least in my opinion—she later joined our dormitory's Mini 500 tricycling team. There she discovered a sporting activity that perfectly favored her four-foot-eleven-inch height.

At the first meeting of the Willkie Little 500 team, I learned that my enthusiasm for the race was matched by an ample group of guys who wanted to race on our men's team. Either that or they showed up for the free pizza. In any case, I was happy to see the activity was co-ed and that some handsome fellows were involved. Unfortunately, there weren't many females excited about racing. Several who showed initial interest would end up disappearing after they learned more about the commitment involved.

An earnest, spiky-haired RA from Mason Hall, Kevin Wentz, took charge of the meeting. Once we had grabbed our slices of pizza, he started in: "OK, so welcome, everyone. I'm Kevin and this—" with his hand, he indicated the blond, rosy-cheeked RA at his side, who flashed us a smile, "is Kristin. So we called this meeting, and we wanted to do it early, because this year we really want people to know about the Little 500. It's a bike race where housing units compete against one another. So it's fraternities versus other fraternities and dorms and independents—people who live off-campus. This year, they're gonna have a women's race. It's the first time. It's a pretty big deal." He paused as if reliving some memory of past Little 500 races. "So, anyway, we want to support it. We want to be there, as a dorm, to have a team of you girls racing in it. We want to have *both*—a men's and a women's team."

Kevin asked, "Has anyone seen the movie *Breaking Away*?" A few of the guys smiled, and their hands went up, but most had not seen the movie.

I did not put my hand up. But someone asked, "Is that the movie with the Cutters?" And I realized that I actually *had* seen the movie years earlier when I was ten or eleven years old. It had been the rare occasion when my entire family had seen a film together in a theater. Rare because of the cost of movie tickets for a family of seven. In fact, we had only done so on that occasion because my brother was a paperboy. The *Wisconsin State Journal* had rented an entire movie theater to treat all its young employees and their families to a free outing. It was the newspaper's way of thanking all the kids who every single day opened a big bundle of newspapers, carefully folded and rubber-banded them (or stuck them in protective plastic sheaths in the case of wet weather), loaded them into big canvas newspaper delivery bags, and hoisted them on, finally armed to walk or bike door-to-door delivering the newspapers to all the subscribing homes.

My older brother PJ had taken on the paper route in our neighborhood when he was twelve years old or so. PJ was lured, as are many preteen route carriers, by the opportunity to make money for the first time. He chose to deliver the *Capital Times*, our city's afternoon paper, basically because he did not want to wake in the wee hours to deliver papers on cold Wisconsin mornings. What he hadn't bargained for was that the *CapTimes* subscribers could also order the thick Sunday edition of the *Wisconsin State Journal*, which was to be delivered by 7:00 a.m. The heft of that Sunday edition added to the insult of waking up at 6:00 on Sunday mornings. It weighed three times that of the afternoon *CapTimes* with all of the publicity and advertising inserts. This was long before the internet, and newspapers provided both the only alternative to waiting till the 6 p.m. news hour on TV and the best way to promote sales. Needless to say, PJ, allergic as he was to waking early, quickly tired of the Sunday morning wake-ups and passed the route off to my brother David.

Our family heritage was a mixture: Irish and Norwegian blood on my mom's side, Polish and German on my dad's. Dave definitely had received the "German blood" in our family (his share and my own!). What I mean is that he was disciplined and hardworking from the start. Dave rocked that paper route for years, consistently reaping the reward of generous tips from his customers for his great service. He was the paperboy supreme right up until he started to have other work options open up, "real jobs" like bussing tables and washing dishes at the busy Crandall's Restaurant on Friday and Saturday nights.

Finally it was my turn—my sister Ann had no interest—and eventually I took over what had become the family paper route. I was a skinny kid, and the weight of the loaded delivery bag overwhelmed my thin frame. I opted to ride my bike to make the paper route go faster. I enjoyed the challenge of learning to balance all my weight to one side on my bike to compensate for the paper bag that seemed to weigh as much as I did. I hoped to eventually master launching perfect tosses from my bike to customers' front porches. Alas, I never did. With the thick canvas cross-strap digging into my shoulder, I was pretty miserable. The weight of the bag made me feel as if I was drowning. I only lasted a few months before passing the route off to my neighborhood buddy Greg, who seemed to have his own share of German blood and kept the route for years.

Anyway, I remembered the fun day watching *Breaking Away* in the Westgate Shopping Mall's cinema—the theater packed with paperboys (no papergirls, if my memory serves) and their families. The homegrown story was perfect for that crowd, which audibly, and sometimes loudly, laughed, sighed, or cheered for the main character, Dave Stohler, and his friends, Moocher, Cyril, and Mike. I had not thought about the story in years, nor had I made the connection to Bloomington until that moment. I remembered Dave Stohler, the earnest main character with his fascination for bicycling and all things Italian, with fondness. I recalled that the film's climax involved a raucous bicycle race pitting the townie Cutters against a preppy team of fraternity boys. The crowd was sizable and cheering loudly. *Ah, so that was the* Little 500 *race*, I thought. For the first time, I was able to visualize what this bike team was about. *Cool.* This was going to be fun.

Kevin explained that his goal after graduation from IU was to become a high school math teacher and basketball coach. "So," he said, "coaching our team, coaching you guys, it's not like they are forcing me to do it because someone, one of us RAs, has to do it. I have always wanted to be a coach, so I am pretty excited about this."

"And I'm telling you guys, I mean, this race, it's really fun to be part of. You won't regret it. But it's also super competitive. People get really into it. So," said Kevin, clearly already savoring the role of coach, "we're going to train. I want to start training this semester." Kevin talked a little more about the race, and I could see why he wanted to coach. He seemed to be naturally imbued with a coach's vernacular and ability to motivate athletes.

We figured out who had bikes. Some had them, some did not, and some had them but had not brought them to college. I pictured my own bike. I loved that bike. I had purchased it three years earlier, during my sophomore year of high school. At the time, my friend Heyhey and I had heard about the new sport called triathlon. We had had fun doing a few 10K runs together, and we were drawn by the challenge of three sports all in one race. Heyhey bought a beautiful celestial Bianchi at the Yellow Jersey bike shop, where we became regulars. I started babysitting more—every weekend night—and saved my money.

Finally one spring day, I had enough. I marched into Yellow Jersey and bought a used Motobecane road bike. With my new ride, I was able to join Heyhey on long rides out into the countryside of America's Dairyland. We signed up for our first triathlon. As the only racers in the female fifteen-to-sixteen age group, we placed first and second. Smiling from the podium, we decided to do another triathlon. And then another. Heyhey posted pictures of Ironman winner Dave Scott in her locker at West High School, and we started regularly riding the twenty-eight miles round trip to Paoli and back after school.

I was worried my Motobecane might get stolen at college, so I sadly left it in my parents' basement, where I imagined it collecting dust. Now that I knew I could keep it in the team's secure bike room, I would get it during the next trip home. I was glad that I had an excuse to bring it to school. And I did just that. After Thanksgiving break, Dad and I loaded it on the hatchback bike rack that we had mounted on the VW Rabbit. He always took the job of securing the bike quite seriously. Off we went with an intricate web of bungee cords locking it in place, just as we had when traveling to the triathlons.

Kevin encouraged us to organize a few rides together, just to start getting out on our bikes. The other RA, Kristin, took the floor: "Hi, everybody. We are so happy that there are a lot of you. I hope it's not just for the pizza! Seriously, this race is a big deal. It will make a difference in your college experience. The women's race, they're really trying to make sure it's a success. It's pretty special. I have been helping them put signs up all over campus, to get enough women to ride. I am glad we have some women here. But . . . it'd be great if you could keep talking up the race to other people." She looked at us, the female contingent at the meeting, pointedly and added: "We need more of you. Tell all your friends about it. It's a commitment, yes, but totally worth it. We are making history in the women's race." We had about five girls at that meeting. I thought, *Well, we only need four riders for the team, so why worry?* But Kristin was right when she had hypothesized: "Someone might quit. Or let's say someone gets injured." Three of the girls vanished after that first meeting, probably not wanting to commit to training all year.

So in a flash, it was down to the RA herself, Kristin McArdle, plus two of us freshmen: Kirsten Swanson and me. Like Kevin, Kirsten lived in Mason Hall, the student apartments affiliated with our dorm quadrangle. Athletic throughout her childhood, Kirsten had also committed from the moment she had heard about the race, and she was all in. Serious and hardworking by nature, Kirsten was already working two jobs. She seemed in some ways wise beyond her years—which was good because we had an immediate problem to solve. Kirsten did not have a bike.

Since Kevin and Kristin insisted that any bike would do, I thought of offering her my old bike, which I had earned when I was around thirteen years old. TV Lenny, owner of a large electronics store and famous in Madison for starring in his own commercials, had offered a free ten-speed bicycle to anyone raising $100 for MS. He announced his fundraising campaign in (where else?) a commercial.

When my sister Molly and I saw it, our eyes grew wide. As the fourth and fifth kids in the family, we had never had new bikes. We picked up the donation forms, and our mission to earn new bikes began. We walked door-to-door for hours, for days, collecting sometimes just $1 at a time from people until we each had reached the $100 mark. We turned our forms and money in at American TV & Appliances and excitedly helped my mom load two brand-new ten-speeds into the trunk of our wood-paneled station wagon. We put a lot of neighborhood miles on those bikes despite our brothers' immediate declaration upon unloading them that the ten-speeds were "total junk." Since my brothers had been right about the dubious quality, I held back on offering that bike to Kirsten.

"It's not like I have much money to buy a bike," Kirsten told me. "I am just lucky to be here, to be at college at all."

"Oh, really? Why?" I asked, assuming that she was barely admitted due to low high school grades or a weak SAT score.

"My parents, they were supposed to have it all covered, because my dad worked for DePauw University. DePauw is one of those schools that pays full college tuition for its professors' kids. At *any* school. I could have gone to the Ivy Leagues, all paid. My friend whose dad works there is going to Brown. Another guy went to Yale." I waited for the reason why she was here and not at Brown herself.

"But then my dad," she said, searching for words, "well, he got fired. Our money for tuition, just gone." Kirsten seemed pretty mad about it still. Understandably.

"Sorry, that's terrible" was all I could think of.

"Yeah, it is," Kirsten responded. "He screwed up. It ended up breaking up our family. It was bad . . ." she trailed off, then finished, "It just really sucked." I winced as the sadness of her story descended on me. She had every reason to be flaming mad. She went from having her tuition covered for any college in the country to facing the possibility of not going at all.

She applied for financial aid. When she received less of it than she expected, her dad told her—at the very last minute, the day they were supposed to drive up to Michigan, with the car already fully loaded—that he could not pay the tuition for her to attend Central Michigan University, where she had been admitted to an undergraduate program in athletic training that interested her.

"Fine," Kirsten had told him in anger, "I am not going to college then. I am just going to start working at the factory. I can walk down there and have a job in five minutes. Then I won't have to rely on you anymore and always end up disappointed." Ouch. I winced at her retelling of the difficult conversation.

"At that point," Kirsten said, "my dad told me that there was no way he was going to let me get a job at the P&G factory in town. That would not be happening. Since the car was already loaded with all my stuff, he drove me

down here instead of up to Michigan. Just like it was the same difference."
She had also been admitted to IU. Her dad took her straight to the registrar's
office and worked some magic. They allowed late enrollment since it was still
the first week of classes. He also managed to secure her a spot in Mason Hall
in the Willkie Quadrangle. He unloaded her belongings and left her on the
front steps as the Mason Hall staff figured out which room to allot to this
last-minute-addition student. What a start to college.

Kirsten handled it well. As she told me about it, her voice never wavered
once. I felt so bad for her, but she spoke about it all pretty matter-of-factly.
She was not one to sit around feeling sorry for herself. Kirsten had emotional
support from her twin sister, Kim, who was also on campus. They were total
opposites in looks and pretty much everything else too. Kim was sweet,
manicured, and more introverted, while Kirsten was competitive, intense,
and loved a good argument. Kirsten saved some tuition money by signing up
for Reserve Officers' Training Corps (ROTC) courses, which were tuition-
free. The US Army offered the free courses to attract students to the full
ROTC program. Kirsten eventually did fully enroll in ROTC. The military
suited her well. Already then, at age eighteen, she had the confidence and
steady voice of a commander. In short, Kirsten was definitely someone you
wanted on your side. She was a survivor, as resilient as they come. She had
strong opinions, and you did not want to disagree with her. For all of those
reasons, Kirsten made a great teammate and a loyal friend. She would become a backbone for our team, as her intensity inspired us all.

But for now, she needed a bike. My new teammate's story touched me. I
wanted to help somehow. A few days later, I went to the Schwinn shop with
her and one of the guys on the dorm team, Joe, who actually had both raced
his bike and followed the sport of cycling. He could help pick out a bike that
met the criteria of (a) being good enough to log some good training miles on
and (b) not costing too terribly much. There, the young manager of the bike
shop, Wes Harris, told us that he had ridden in the Little 500 for the past few
years for his team, called the Posers. We smiled at the name. Cycling, with
all the sport-specific gear and clothing, did seem to attract a fair number of
posers. He wanted to help out and offered Kirsten some great deals on what
he had there. We left with a little sheet of paper listing the bikes and prices.
Kirsten called him a few days later to ask if he would put aside one of the bikes

until she had enough money to pay it off. A few weeks later, she was riding a brand-new Schwinn road bike around.

Kevin and Kristin had instructed us to work on rider recruitment. I tried to talk a few friends on my dorm floor into giving the team a try. Cindy Nixon, a redhead from Ann Arbor, Michigan, who was always quick to laugh, lived just kitty-corner down the hallway. I talked up the team to her, since I knew she had done some sports in high school. She came to one meeting but in the end lasted just a few weeks before giving it up. Eventually though, by the end of that first semester, she passed the torch to Louise Elder, who was her quieter and more reserved roommate from Louisville, Kentucky.

Louise was up for the challenge and poured her heart into our workouts. But she also realized that she was on a strong team athletically and felt a bit insecure about her own ability. Louise had done a bicycle tour with her family a year earlier, so she felt comfortable on a bike, but she had not participated in sports much.

"I am not sure that I can do this. I mean, you guys are so good—maybe I am just not athletic enough," Louise told me one day as we walked back from an indoor workout. From that point on, we started to go on some rides, just the two of us. I wanted to help her develop her skills without feeling pressured. On those rides, she could take things at her own pace without feeling like the weak link. We chatted and became better friends. I was no expert, but I gave her all the tips that I could think of. I told her that it did not matter at all if she was not our strongest athlete. She had heart. Anything she lacked in pure athleticism, Louise made up for with her enthusiasm and never-give-up attitude.

Kristin, the RA of the sixth floor in Willkie North tower, was in her junior year. A friend of the 1987 Kappa Alpha Theta team, Kristin wanted to help make sure the women's race was a success. She had been at the Little 500 track to cheer on her Theta friends in their attempt to make history the previous year. Kristin had been the one to post the callout signs all over our dormitory. She was directly involved with the efforts to make the women's race a reality and was working with the IUSF, the student foundation that had been created by Howdy Wilcox Jr. and had ever since been the organizer of the Little 500 race. Kristin decided to race herself and was doing everything in her power to make sure that Willkie had a team on race day. She had been captain of both her swim and track teams in high school. Her encouragement for the rest of us never wavered, and she backed it up with her organizational prowess, getting us a small budget and bike room in the dorm.

Kristin's maturity stood out with respect to the fresh-out-of-high-school rest of us. She was from Boston and brought her East Coast crispness to our group. Her strawberry blonde hair and freckled complexion were matched by her sunny personality. Kristin was our team's shiniest member and also our most dedicated. She attended all of the organizational meetings with Kevin but also all of our practices on the bike. Kristin was not distracted like we were by being in the first semester away from home, and she was continually working behind the scenes on our behalf.

Kristin had a broader vision of what the race meant than the rest of us riders. Two members of the 1987 Kappa Alpha Theta team who were part of the unsuccessful qualifying attempt for the men's race had graduated. However, two remained. Joined by some new sorority teammates, they hoped to take part in the race that they had created. Worried that there would not be enough interest among students to create a deep field of teams, the Theta riders worked tirelessly in that first semester to get the word out about the race and to spur interest among women on campus. As a result of the Thetas' well-publicized attempt to enter the men's race the previous year, a core group of their supporters, friends, and sorority sisters had volunteered to help recruit enough teams to make the women's race both a reality and a success. Luckily, they also had the support of IUSF's young assistant director, Spero Pulos, who helped the students organize and hold meetings all around campus to ensure the success of the inaugural women's race.

Kristin was also in their ranks. The IUSF and the Theta riders had drawn her in to help recruit at the dorms all over campus. Kristin canvassed the dorms with signs and helped at informational meetings. She instructed dorms that it was best to have a team of seven or eight riders in case some did not make it through the coming months. It was her personal mission to ensure that Willkie would field a team. After turning over every rock, we only had four potential riders. She assured us that we could make it fine with four because we were all dedicated. Our team was complete.

Or so we thought. Just after Christmas break, Kirsten ran into her best friend from elementary school, Amy Tucker. They bumped into one another in the parking lot of Assembly Hall, the home arena of our prized and winning IU Hoosier basketball team and its antic-filled coach Bobby Knight.

How can I help myself from writing a side note about Bobby? He was famous for being one of the winningest college basketball coaches of all time but infamous for his temper, which often led to outrageous acts, usually directed at officials or reporters. Sometimes even at his own players. Once, mad about a referee's call, Knight famously grabbed a chair from the IU bench and threw it across the court, for which he was promptly ejected from the game. This incident had provided the name for my favorite bakery, due to their amazing chocolate chip cookies: the Red Chair Bakery. Bobby Knight had coached the Hoosiers to the NCAA championship in the year before I arrived on campus. It was IU's fifth national championship banner and Knight's third as IU coach. In the basketball-loving state of Indiana, Bobby Knight was a god. His controversial behavior became more pronounced, and years later, long after I had graduated, he was fired. Everyone is held accountable for their actions eventually. But during my tenure at IU, Knight was king.

Amy and Kirsten's friendship went way back to their days of attending the same elementary school in Greencastle, Indiana, where they grew up. As kids, they used to meet up at the neighborhood skateboard ramp or in the woods between their two homes. They were best friends for many of their younger years. They competed on sports teams together—and against one another—during those years. In eighth grade, Kirsten moved away after her parents' difficult split. She and Amy lost touch during their high school years.

In our freshman year, Amy joined the IU Cross Country team as a walk-on athlete. She was strong enough to earn a spot, but unfortunately, she had been plagued by injury all fall and had not been able to compete in a single race. With no healing from her injuries in sight, Amy was frustrated, and she reluctantly decided to leave the team. As fate had it, literally just moments after Amy met with her cross-country coach in Assembly Hall and withdrawn from the team, she bumped into Kirsten.

Upon hearing Amy's tale of woe, Kirsten quipped, "Join our Little 500 team! We need another rider."

"Sounds fun, but I don't even have a bike," said Amy.

"I didn't either. Get one!" Kirsten told Amy about the race and urged her to join us in the Little 500.

Amy hopped in her car and drove off. But the next day, she showed up at our Willkie bike team meeting. In their serendipitous encounter that day, Kirsten had essentially recruited Amy on the spot. Amy joined the team, and we were happy to have her. She was game to jump in and try a new sport. She went right out and bought herself a bike. In no time, Amy was driving around with a bike protruding awkwardly from the trunk of her black Trans Am.

I was surprised at the Trans Am. Really I think it was part of an across-the-board culture shock that I experienced in Indiana. Up in Madison, my high school friends and I were driving around in Volvos, VWs, and Saabs—especially since we were teens driving our parents' cars around. Maybe a car that seemed cool in our eyes would have been a BMW.

Honestly, in 1987, it was somewhat rare to have a car as a college freshman at all. But Amy had one, and she'd chosen a Trans Am? Not only that, it was the Firebird Trans Am with the huge golden firebird decal on the long front hood. In other words, it was a classic muscle car. Those sorts of differences between my Indiana classmates and my friends from Madison, my ultra-progressive hometown, gave me the sense that I was out of my element down in south central Indiana. The Southern twang in the accent was another. Amy had that too.

Amy's misfortune with the IU cross-country team, her running injuries, translated to our team's good fortune. She was a determined and strong athlete, with a big and contagious laugh. We would soon discover that her sprint was a powerful addition for us. So was her attitude. Hopping out of her muscle car, Amy might appear intimidating, like someone you would not want to cross. In time though, I learned that she was just a bit shy. Once she got to know you and you were in her circle, she might immediately offer a wisecrack or self-deprecating comment upon exiting her Trans Am and follow it up with a hearty laugh. Athletically, she was formidable, seemingly made of all fast-twitch muscle that gave her a deadly sprint. I could see why she and Kirsten were friends—both had a passion and talent for sports and a never-say-die attitude. The physical talent of those two could just make us a force to be reckoned with. Our team was now truly complete.

Finally, we had managed to field a team five riders deep, and it was a strong one at that. Amy, Kirsten, Kristin, and I had been dedicated high school athletes in multiple sports. Louise rounded out our gritty athleticism with pure enthusiasm. We were all pretty good on the bike too.

CHAPTER

IN LATE FALL, the Thetas and other female riders who had taken part in the Little 500 Series events in the previous year offered training advice to teams. They were joined by Spero, the IUSF assistant director who had been a rider in the men's race as a student. Sessions were organized with interested riders. We partook in one such session in Dunn Meadow, the expansive grassy field on the edge of campus reserved for student activities and rallies. We showed up on bikes, as did one of the sorority teams. It was a gray day with humidity that made it feel even colder. We were greeted by several riders who seemed expertly bundled up against the cold.

After introducing themselves, while we all shivered and rubbed our hands together to stay warm, these riders told us that they were really excited that the race had garnered so much interest, that many of us wanted to take part in it. They went on to say that the session was designed to help teams learn how to get ready for being part of Little 500. Finally, so we would not get cold hanging around talking too much, they went over a few basics about the race and offered guidance about how to prepare for it.

We learned that the race would take place on a cinder track, a big oval around the soccer field at the Bill Armstrong Stadium. Since the soccer season was underway, we were not able to practice on the track until springtime. The riders explained that there were four riders per team on race day. It was essentially run like a relay race, where individual team members had to pass off the bike to each other.

What was most important about the session that day was learning exactly how to pass off the bike to one another—what was known as the infamous "bike exchange." Apparently this exchange was kind of tricky. The idea was to practice it a bit—to start learning it right then in the fall semester—so riders would be ready when the track opened in the spring. Exchanging knowing smiles, the experienced riders told us that we wanted to crash—and apparently there was no doubt that we would crash—on the grass and not on the track. They all grimaced at the memory of taking spills on the track. I summoned up my own visual: the skinned and scabbed knees that had accompanied me through my entire childhood.

The easiest thing was to just demonstrate how this exchange was done and have us try doing it ourselves. Then when we had some nicer days during winter, we could find a flat field where we could practice on our own.

One of the riders instructing us walked away down the field a bit and crouched down, looking back toward us over her shoulder. Her partner rode toward the crouching rider, and I witnessed my first bike exchange: As the rider on the bike approached, the crouched rider started running away from her, keeping her right arm extended out to the side as she sprinted down the field. As she ran away from us and the oncoming bicycle, she occasionally peered over her shoulder to keep her eye on the approaching rider. The cyclist rode straight toward the outstretched arm and then seemed to jump from the bike, which the sprinting rider in turn grabbed and hopped on to. It was quite a feat. We asked to see it again and then again another time.

Then it was our turn. We shivered through attempted exchanges all afternoon in Dunn Meadow, with some epic falls and a lot of laughter—and occasionally, just occasionally, a spark of understanding about how it felt to do one right. With the patience of saints, our instructing riders encouraged my teammates and me as we either raced by our teammates too fast or stopped too early, causing them to lose momentum entirely or even run back for the bike.

Later that week, we watched the videotape that Kevin and the other coaches had been given. It was specially made for the new coaches and new teams, to help them instruct their riders on how to perform exchanges. There were some slow-motion exchanges. Step by step, exchanges go like this: You pull out from the inner track toward your team's "pit" zone—cruising full speed toward the right of your waiting teammate, who breaks into a sprint upon your arrival. You step on the right-side pedal to slow your bike using its coaster brakes. Keeping the bike steady, you stand on the right pedal while simultaneously lifting your foot off the left pedal. Finally you let go of first the left and then the right handlebar as you step off the bike. Performed well, the bike barely slows and hardly wavers during the exchange. It maintains continuous motion, gliding on its own for a moment toward your sprinting teammate, who then grabs it by the stem. Taking hold of the handlebars solidly, she gives her sprint its final kick and launches her legs off the ground for an airborne moment that finishes with her bum landing on the seat and her feet swinging onto the pedals. The exchange is usually followed up by an immediate sprinting effort to get up to speed and catch back on to the moving pack of cyclists.

There are approximately a thousand different ways that an exchange can become a disaster. Did I mention that the experienced riders who patiently taught us that day in Dunn Meadow had made exchanges look easy? On the few nice days remaining that fall, we worked to master our bike exchanges on the grassy lawn behind Mason Hall. I saw other teams out too, practicing exchanges on grassy fields and lawns around campus. During one of our practice sessions, I raced toward Louise, who had her knees bent as she waited to start her sprint. She took off as I approached, but our timing was off. She stopped and restarted to try to get back in sync with me. Only it was too late. We watched with dismay as the bike headed toward her like a missile, moving much quicker than she was. As she grabbed at the stem, the bike wavered, and the back wheel reared up to smack her in the back. She yelled and fell. There was a silent moment as we waited to hear that she was OK. As she rose from the fall and untangled herself from the bike, Louise had an epiphany: "I think our strategy should be to do as few exchanges as possible, y'all agree?" We all burst into laughter—and agreed with her, heartily.

We did give up working on exchanges, as Kevin made the executive decision that we'd wait until the track opened to do that. Instead, he'd decided, it was time to turn up the notch on our training. In late fall and early winter, the weather was cold and often rainy. After my classes, I spent a lot of time meeting up with the others in the afternoon or evening to train in the team's bike room. We had been given a space in the men's tower of our dorm, Willkie South, where we could congregate to train. There we had equipment such as bicycle trainers and rollers as well as mats and a few free weights.

While waiting for the weather to warm up and dry up so we could get out on the open roads, my teammates and I learned how to ride bicycle rollers through trial and error. Or should I say trial and crash? Rollers consist of three cyclical drums within a frame, with a rubber belt connecting the front and rear cylinders. Balancing carefully, you ride your bicycle on top of the rollers. Just as a treadmill moves under you as you walk or run on top of it, the rollers rotate endlessly to simulate the road under your front and rear wheels, only that in the case of rollers, it is your pedaling that keeps the rollers moving. Since you are not fixed in position, it sort of feels like riding on the open road.

Riding rollers was very freeing compared to riding the wind trainers to which you attached to your back wheel. Until it was not . . . because you had fallen off. One challenge with riding rollers is that you must maintain your focus. If you turn your gaze away to the side instead of focusing directly in front of you, often your body naturally veers that way and you ride right off the side of the rollers. It truly simulates riding on a very narrow strip of road, where going off the road means crashing hard. Being trapped by the leather strap cinched down on your pedals' toe clips and without enough time to react and clip out, you can take a devastating fall as you go from a healthy speed on rollers—they are most stable if you are doing at least 80–90 rpm—to zero when you touch down. Down in the bike room, we took some epic spills. We soon learned to clear anything with sharp edges from the potential fall zone before we started up our roller sessions to protect ourselves.

These were the days of cassette tape players. We turned the music up loud and pedaled away to our mixtapes featuring recent hits by U2, Bruce Springsteen, Prince, INXS, The Cure, Sting, Squeeze, and John Cougar Mellencamp. And of course, the Queen song "Bicycle Race."

Born and raised in Indiana, John Mellencamp lived just outside of Bloomington. His record label had forced him to produce his first records under the name John Cougar, chosen to match how his New York record label perceived his down-home Indiana persona. His music was centered around the stories and the lives of ordinary people. He sang about those living in America's Heartland. After garnering enough clout and success to produce under his own name, he evolved to using his own last name and put his albums out under the name John Cougar Mellencamp, eventually dropping "Cougar" altogether. Like any hometown superstar, Mellencamp was a local legend.

Mellencamp was mostly a quiet presence in Bloomington. Occasionally though, he would show up unannounced to play live at a local bar. That first happened during my tenure in Bloomington a few weeks after the semester started. On my dorm floor, Shelly from down the hall got a late-night call from her upperclassman boyfriend telling her that Mellencamp was playing live at the Bluebird, a local bar that often had live music. Shelly was apparently out the door in seconds. I did not hear about it until an hour later when I ran into her roommate while I was brushing my teeth in the bathroom. I was certain that news of Mellencamp playing live had spread like wildfire and there was no chance of getting into the Bluebird anymore. Even back in those days before cell phones existed, big news traveled fast. There would be a rush on the nearest pay phone. People called their friends, who in turn called their friends, and so on. The bar would quickly fill to capacity. Fans would gather in a long line outside the door, but of course there was no hope of actually getting in as no one would ever exit those jam sessions. That particular night, there were a few special guests, Lou Reed and John Prine, who were in town visiting Mellencamp before they headed to the Farm Aid III concert. Shelly had not gotten in, but she was thrilled to have heard the concert from the line on the sidewalk, including Lou Reed belting out "Hey babe, take a walk on the wild side."[6]

One day just before Christmas break, I went over to the bike room solo to get in an evening workout on the rollers. I stuck in a mixed tape, turned it up loud, and got myself going on the rollers to Yaz's "Only You." I focused on the cycling poster portraying Greg LeMond on the wall in front of me and did some high-rpm spinning intervals. I paid no attention to the guys who passed by on their way to the laundry room, but in my peripheral vision, I eventually saw someone with a laundry basket lingering at the open door for a bit. I wondered if the blaring music was perhaps too loud for someone. Despite the tricky act of looking to the side and simultaneously staying steady on the rollers, I gave a quick glance toward the figure in the doorway.

"Hey," said a guy I recognized from our men's bike team. Essentially the men's and women's teams had been carrying out their training separately, and we had not had too much contact with one another since that first meeting.

"Seems like a good idea. Maybe I'll come join you," he said before walking off with his full laundry basket. I hoped that he would. Robert, I recalled him saying his name was when we all introduced ourselves at that meeting. He seemed nice enough, and he was certainly good-looking—with chocolatey eyes and dark hair that was gathered in a ponytail. I became a little self-conscious about how profusely I was sweating. The bike room was always overheated as it was located between the heating system and the laundry room on the ground floor of the men's tower. Did I smell? Of course I did. I was working out after all! Wasn't I supposed to be sweaty and smelly? I continued my intervals, performing them full-throttle, even more motivated at the prospect that Robert might show up. And he did.

"Hey, do you work at the cafeteria?" he asked as he entered. I finished my final interval and then drank a long slurp from my water bottle before answering yes. I kept riding the rollers, taking it easy now for my cooldown. Sweat dripped from every pore, so Robert was unlikely to notice my blushing at the mention of my cafeteria job. For whatever reason, having been recognized as a cafeteria worker embarrassed me. I had taken the job for a little spending cash and only worked two breakfast shifts per week, reloading food as students depleted various items. I never came to breakfast on the days that I did not work, preferring instead to sleep every last second possible before waking for my classes. I was glad to see that most others also skipped that meal since I did not fancy waiting on or serving my classmates much. Luckily, I rarely saw anyone I knew.

"Yeah, I am pretty sure that you served me peaches the other day," Robert said, and I turned redder, although I was certain he could not distinguish that from the effect of my sprints. I was usually pretty sleepy on my morning shift, maxing out my ZZZs and waking up approximately ten minutes before I had to be on the job. But still, it seemed unlikely that I could have served him without recognizing him. He was dark and handsome. Trust me, I would have remembered seeing him. For sure. I would have been interested. Anyway, that morning, I had just scooped peaches into small dishes and placed them out for people to grab. It would be a stretch to say that I had "served" them to anyone.

"Huh. I am pretty out of it in the mornings. But yeah, I did scoop peaches. Sorry, I didn't see you," I responded.

He hopped on a trainer and started riding. We chatted as he warmed up and I warmed down. He had a faded Beatles T-shirt on. I told him that I listened to them a lot. To me, the Beatles represented musical genius. In any case though, I loved anything classic, stuff that had stood the test of time, music or anything else. Every mixtape I made had at least one Beatles tune on it. Rob told me that his brother had printed and framed the lyrics to "Imagine" as his Christmas present. Check, for him and one for his brother too. Eventually I hopped off the trainer, toweled off, and did some stretching while he amped up his workout. I finished up and walked back to my dorm giddy from our exchange. Starting then, I spent just a little bit more time on making myself presentable on the mornings that I worked in the Willkie cafeteria.

CHAPTER

WHILE HOME AT CHRISTMAS BREAK, I excitedly told my family about the Little 500 race. My brother Dave remembered *Breaking Away* and teased me about being a Cutter. My dad, an associate dean of the College of Letters and Science at the University of Wisconsin, was more interested in how my classes were going and whether I was keeping my nose to the grindstone. Once I was able to quell that concern—I had, in fact, done well—he and the others wanted to know: Did the Cutters still exist? What kind of track do you race on? Are the corners banked?

I realized that I really did not know as much about the race as I thought I did. I told them what I did know: That my teammates were pretty cool. That bike exchanges were hard because you tried not to lose any time on the pack while you literally passed a moving bike. That we would be issued a

Roadmaster race bike with coaster brakes, made by Huffy (another chance for my brothers to tell me that I was riding a "piece of crap" bike). That I had learned to ride rollers.

Actually, I wished that I had brought the rollers home! Every day over that break, I put on my running shoes, bundled up against the Wisconsin cold, and ran the five miles along the lakefront from our home to the governor's mansion and back. One motivation for going south for college was the weather. I loved being with my family, but I couldn't wait to head back down to school and leave the cold behind.

Just after we arrived back on campus, Kevin called a meeting and told us it was time to turn it up a notch on training. Wes Harris, the Schwinn employee who had helped Kirsten and, just recently, Amy get their bikes, had befriended our team. Wes had offered to lead us through some indoor workouts at the shop while he was working. Amy, Kirsten, and I showed up one afternoon and set up on trainers among the shiny new bikes and cycling clothing on display. We warmed up and did some longer efforts. Then Wes got us doing some intervals.

"Gotta do stuff like this to build speed and endurance," he told us. To motivate us, he had us envision a race scenario.

"OK, we are doing our last one," he said as we started our final thirty-second interval. "Five . . . four . . . three . . . two . . . one. Go! Go! It's your last one! Picture this: The leader of the race is just in front of you, but she has opened up a gap. Twenty-three seconds left! It's the last chance you might have to stay with her. You are losing her! Eighteen seconds . . . Come on, don't let her get away! Go! Go! Go! Twelve seconds . . . Come on, faster! Come on! Catch that wheel! Eight seconds, six, five . . ." I was sweating and turning my legs over as fast as seemed humanly possible at that moment. *Catch her!* I shouted to myself, only in my head. Suddenly though, I felt something shift in my belly. Oh no, it was my lunch, coming up. I quickly brought my feet to a halt, loosened my toe clips on the pedals, and ran outside the shop door to the parking lot. The cold hit me like a wall, and chills overtook my shaky body. I threw up, right there outside the entrance to the shop. Amy had followed me outside. "You OK?" she asked. Then as Kirsten arrived, "She threw up, Kirsten, watch out!"

"Jeezus," Kirsten responded. "Can I just say something? Can I just point out that maybe we are taking this training a little too seriously? Pushing ourselves a little too hard? I'm just saying. Kevin and Wes, they don't realize how serious we take this stuff."

All I could muster in response was, "That's the *last time* I will be eating our cafeteria pizza. Never again." We laughed and headed back in to do our warm-down.

Before long, spring brought a more interesting alternative to sweating up a storm in the bike shop or bike room. The allure of riding on actual roads overtook us as the amount of daylight increased, the temperatures warmed, and the air became less frigid. We took our first forays outdoors. I found that Mellencamp's lyrics had been a fitting introduction to the country roads outside of Bloomington. It was easy to see why he was inspired by these woodsy rolling hills. Riding through Monroe, Brown, and Morgan Counties in central Indiana, I trained hard but also loved the chance to see the splendor of the local countryside. Glaciers had left the northern part of the state with very flat terrain, but they had not extended this far south. The territory surrounding Bloomington had developed into rolling hills and thick green forests due to the rock and debris left behind when the glacier melted.

Our fitness progressed as we got out into the hills surrounding Bloomington. Powering ourselves up and down them provided a new level of endurance that we had not been able to achieve with our indoor training. We watched our leg muscles grow and strengthen. Our rides provided me with a tour of the small-town America that I had never really known. I felt like I might come upon the house featured in the music video for Mellencamp's song "Pink Houses." I was certain that any one of the communities I passed through could be where the love ballad telling "the little ditty about Jack and Diane" originated. We rode through town after town with enclaves of small homes and modest yards. This was the territory that inspired "Small Town." I came to understand why Mellencamp was a hometown hero, as big a star as anyone who didn't play basketball in Indiana could be. Everyone hoped to catch one of his impromptu rock sessions at the local bars. Unfortunately, I never did.

The timing of the Indiana monsoon season was not great for Little 500 athletes. April showers bring May flowers, so they say. The spectacular foliage and beautiful flowers all over the IU campus only came as the prize for enduring a whole lot of spring rain, and it did not start in April in Bloomington. You were guaranteed to get some good use of your umbrella in January, February, and March too. Trudging to class was quite the wet business. It didn't take long before my roommate, Karen, and I took a shopping trip for umbrellas and waterproof shoes. Karen bought rubber rain boots, seemingly an essential item for surviving the Bloomington spring.

Bundling up well against the dampness and cold, the team began taking training rides whenever the weather permitted. Or should I say whenever it wasn't raining. Inevitably my teammates and I would get caught in the rain and return like bedraggled cats with our tails between our legs and a stripe of dirt up our backs—the telling cyclist trademark left by the spray of the rear wheel. The beauty of youth is that we were not really bothered by the rainy weather so much. We came to realize that there was a reason cyclists wore black. Upon our return, the stuffy bike room where we stored our dripping bicycles never felt better. Shivering cold, we might linger a moment in the heat to stretch our cold muscles or add a few sit-ups to warm ourselves up. Then we headed off to our rooms, where we would peel off the soaking wet layers of adherent cycling gear and finally indulge in long hot showers.

One day, we came back dripping to find our seemingly wiser men's team riding indoors. We chatted and stretched a bit while they pedaled away on trainers. When the others headed toward showers, I lingered behind. I had not seen Robert much since we had returned from winter break. I was compelled to stay and strike up a conversation with him as he and Joe continued their workout. It turned out that they were talking about going to Indianapolis that weekend. Joe had a car. Since he was from Indy and needed to go home, Robert planned to join him and see, as Joe put it, "the great city of Indianapolis."

"You wanna come? Kirsten's coming too. Her mom lives up there," Joe offered. As luck would have it, my best friend, Margie, had called the day before to say she had a swim meet in Indianapolis. Margie had stayed in Madison after high school since she had earned a scholarship to swim for the University of Wisconsin. That weekend, she and the UW team would be swimming at the newly built IU Natatorium, and she had asked if I could get there to meet up. Joe's offer would give me the opportunity to see her swim. I might also get to know Robert. I skipped back to my room and called up Margie.

"I'm coming to your swim meet, girlfriend!" I announced to Margie's answering machine, this being long before the advent of cell phones and the modern moment of being ever-reachable. "Found a ride. The IU pool is super fast. I want to witness you getting a PR, baby! See you Saturday."

As Dad and I passed Indianapolis when he drove me down to Blooming-ton a few months earlier, he told me about the pool that had been completed a few years prior. At forty-nine years old, my dad—who had swum on the University of Chicago swim team back in college—was still competing as an active age-group swimmer. Half our family vacations were planned around him participating in the national championships, an open water swim, or some other important swim meet. When he told me that the pool in Indianapolis was "fast" and records had been falling there, I suggested that the pool length came up short: "How else can it be a 'fast pool'?" So Dad explained swimming pool dynamics. The deeper a swimming pool was, the longer it took for the turbulence created by swimming to reach the bottom and ricochet back as surface waves, which slowed swimmers down. The IU Natatorium was deep enough to dampen out that water movement and eliminate choppi-ness. "It's kind of like the effect of riding in someone's slipstream," said Dad, appealing to an example from triathlon in which drafting on the bicycling segment was prohibited.

"Oh I bet ole Doc Counsilman has something to do with that pool being so fast," my dad said, referring to the legendary IU (and also multiple-time Olympic) swim coach who had won even more national championship ban-ners than Bobby Knight. Dad had already told me about Doc Counsilman, who some years earlier had become the oldest person to have ever swum the English Channel at fifty-eight years old. As a long-distance open-water swimmer, my dad had considered giving the Channel crossing a shot himself. Being coached by Counsilman was an achievement in itself, and that fall on campus, I learned that the IU swimmers could be identified by their team T-shirts with "What's up, Doc?" printed on the upper right rear shoulder out of reverence for their famous coach.

That Saturday, Joe, Kirsten, Rob, and I headed up to Indy. We headed out early, and I mostly listened as they discussed jazz and the superiority of Eu-ropean bicycle frames such as Colnago and Masi. Clearly a morning person, Kirsten chirped away from the passenger seat about what she was learn-ing in her nutrition course and how we should eat for the best performance results. Common knowledge of the day was that carbo-loading, eating meals comprised of primarily carbohydrates, such as a big plate of spaghetti, in the period leading up to a race was the best preparation for endurance sports. We had our first races coming up during the following weeks: the events of the Little 500 Series. We were nervous and excited to see how it went. She was making the argument that we needed to start watching what we ate carefully.

Suddenly, Kirsten turned to Rob and me and said, "Oh, I forgot, you guys don't know! Amy got hit by a car yesterday."

That woke me up. "What?! Is she OK? What happened?"

Kirsten told us that she and Amy were supposed to take a ride together. Kirsten had been waiting for her to show up when Amy appeared, with a sheriff following her. Apparently, Amy had been hit, flipped over her handlebars, and landed on the car's hood, which she dented with her head and face. She had not been wearing a helmet, because, well, not too many people did back then. She had a stocking cap on. Embarrassed, Amy told the sheriff who arrived that she was fine. He followed behind her in his squad car anyway, and when she stopped at Mason Hall to meet Kirsten, the sheriff got out. Kirsten told him that Amy did not seem to be her usual self. They started questioning her and found Amy was not able to answer basic questions. They ended up calling an ambulance. It turned out that she had a concussion and had to lay low for a week. We decided to visit her later.

When we arrived in Indianapolis, Kirsten, Joe, and Rob dropped me off at the IU Natatorium, where I would meet Margie. I hoped to witness her breaking some records, even if they were just her own. I saw her swim two events and in between was able to sit and chat with her about life. We hadn't really seen much of each other that year and so had not been able to speak much. Communication was different in 1988. There were no cell phones. Local calls were cheap, but long-distance calls—those to someone outside your three-digit area code—cost you much more. If you had a calling card, it could be cheaper, but the upshot was that you generally were not in touch with folks who were not local. Not as much, for certain. With a calling card, you had to dial in about twenty numbers to be connected, and it was definitely a bit of a hassle. So, reuniting with friends in person held its charm.

Margie had not been home in Madison during winter break as she had gone on the UW swim team's training trip to Hawaii, so we had not seen one another essentially since summer. From a pair of seats in the stands overlooking the races, we shared our news, lots of stories, and giggles with one another. Then she was off to get focused for her next race.

Margie was training hard as an athlete in an NCAA Division I program, and she both loved and was challenged by the intensity. I watched her smooth, powerful strokes as she swam to her best times of the season. One of the coaches walked alongside the swimmers, down the length of the pool as they swam, carefully timing a loud "Sprint! . . . Sprint! . . . Sprint!" for the swimmer to hear each time she turned her head to the side to breathe. The scene inspired me. I vowed to finely tune my body and make riding my bike look as easy as she did powering past her adversaries with those deft strokes.

In the late afternoon, my Willkie friends showed up to get me. Rob ran into the natatorium to find me. As I saw him approach, I recognized that he had a natural aura of "cool." I wasn't sure if it was the long locks (or maybe the related ability to make what was really kind of a mullet so good-looking), his crisp white tee contrasting his dark complexion, or his even-handed friendliness, but he was cool. I was sorry that Margie and Rob could not meet. She had already finished her last event, showered, and headed off with her team. I was happy to see Rob approach, which he did wearing an apologetic smile.

"Sorry we are late. I kept telling them we had to go," he said.

Truth be told, I was relieved that they had arrived—and not just because I could leave the stuffy natatorium, overheated as it was to keep the swimmers warm. I was happy to see them, these new college friends. "No problem," I answered, and we exited together.

Joe and Kirsten took us on a brief tour of Indy's Monument Circle and downtown, and then we headed back down to Bloomington. I told them about Margie's races, animating the relay race in which she had been the final swimmer. I had watched her take the final turn and, starting in second place, manage to catch and decisively out-touch the other racer to win the event.

"And that is exactly how our one-hundred-lap relay will finish—with a little luck on our side," Kirsten said cheerfully after I finished. She, of course, was referring to the one hundred laps of the Little 500.

When we got back to Bloomington, we drove straight to Amy's apartment. Her roommate was out, and Amy answered the door herself. I was shocked to see that the left side of her face was black and blue.

"Looking like a champ, girl," Kirsten said as we entered.

Amy laughed and answered, "Yeah, well, I look better than when I puked all over myself on the X-ray table yesterday! The guy had to clean it all up. I felt so bad about it."

"Ewww," I said.

"Don't feel bad," Joe said. "At least you didn't have to clean it up. That woulda been worse."

"We all have to wear helmets. You could have been really hurt," said Rob. Back at the dorm later, we found out that Kristin and Kevin had already made the shopping trip that day. We all had new helmets waiting for us in the bike room.

After we left Amy's place and parked at our quadrangle, Joe and Kirsten headed back to Mason Hall together, while Rob and I headed toward our Willkie towers. We were silent a beat, and then I asked, "It seems like those two are dating?" Kirsten had not mentioned it, but their behavior that day made it clear that there was something between them.

Rob confirmed, "Yup, I guess so." Then as we reached the North tower, where we would go our separate ways, he asked if I would go to dinner with him sometime.

I felt myself flush and gave a quick, "Sure." I was elated as I headed up to the eleventh floor.

The sunshine started to show up a bit more, and we were slowly able to dress with fewer layers of clothing on our rides. We started to get to know the roads and develop our favorites—this ride might have more climbing, that one a great descent, and another a stretch on a beautiful road. Our favorite became the thirty-mile spin to Lake Lemon and back. Kevin left us to train autonomously for the most part; he saw that we were pretty highly motivated. He just told us to make sure that we kept nudging up our ride distance, building our endurance so that when the Little 500 track opened, we would have a solid base and could focus on speed.

One thing that helped our speed on those road rides: dogs. We had quickly learned that home protection on south central Indiana's country roads was placed in the paws of rabid dogs. The moment they saw or heard us approach, these four-legged security guards turned their full attention on the cyclist visitors. They came sprinting toward us at full speed and frothing at the mouth. *Do we look that tasty?* I thought. As they chased us down, we sometimes tried to deepen our voices to husky male tenor tones and yell out a strong, "No!" in response to their barking. These were mean dogs. Multiple times, my riding companions were nipped on the ankles. I whipped my bicycle frame pump off and swung it at the aggressors on more than a few occasions. But I quickly learned that the best weapon was speed. You just had to ride like hell. Or, well, as if a dog would bite you if you did not outride it first. I was sort of afraid that the dogs would cause me to crash (and who knows what? eat me alive?), so that was even more motivation to hightail it out of their range. It did not occur to me then, but maybe those dogs provided our best speed training.

CHAPTER

I WAS TAKING AN English honors seminar titled Imagining Nature that second semester, taught by Professor Scott Sanders. When I saw the seminar title in the course listings, enrolling was a no-brainer. I had fully inherited my parents' strong reverence for the natural world. In my opinion, there was no better place on earth than the tiny but majestic Sunday Lake up in Northern Wisconsin, where my grandpa had built a cabin in the 1950s. To our family's good fortune, Dad had inherited the place. With five kids, the best vacation is a free one, and we spent our summer weekends and the entire month of July living lake cabin life. There, the only things to do with your time involve engaging with nature.

We spent entire days on the pier, only running up the birch bark stairs to the cabin to use the bathroom or help Mom prepare the picnic lunch; our arms would be filled with sandwiches, potato salad, and sliced watermelon as we marched right back down to eat on the pier. We swam in the sparkling clear water for hours—playing king of the raft or swimming out to the islands and back—only to follow that up with canoeing to the farther away Froggy Island or to see the herons. We shared Sunday Lake with very few humans but many others from nature's kingdom, including turtles, loons, beavers, and bald eagles. With the five of us Hellmuth kids born in just a seven-year span (yup, you guessed it, Catholic), we did not need a TV (which was good since there wasn't one), a telephone (also missing by design), or anything else really aside from my mom's hearty cooking (she never failed us there). Our daily adventures included using the net to catch minnows for fishing, racing each other in swimming triangles from pier to island to point and back to pier, and camping on one of the islands overnight. And about a million other things. Nature illuminated our days, as s'mores, stargazing, and endless card games did our nights.

Professor Sanders had put together a syllabus rich with talented writers, each applying exemplary literary talent toward imagining nature. As we started in with Henry David Thoreau's *Walden*, Sanders read the lines my mom had often quoted to us up on the pier at Sunday Lake:

> I went to the woods because I wished to live deliberately, to front only the essential facts of life, and see if I could not learn what it had to teach, and not, when I came to die, discover that I had not lived.

I had those lines memorized and repeated them silently to myself as he read. They struck a chord with me and not only because I had been raised on them.

Scott Sanders had the rare quality in a professor of listening as much as he spoke. He presented us with authors whose language was as magnificent as any you could find, and then he let us react. When we began our discussion in class, it was as if Professor Sanders was being careful *not* to tell us how to interpret the words we read or indicate in any way how we should respond to them, so as not to spoil the fun part for us. In contrast to a typical lecturer who stood at the front and presented a clean package of literature and its interpretation all wrapped up in one, Scott Sanders would read a passage and ask what we felt about it. At times, he sat down at one of the student desks, right there next to us, inciting us to share our responses to that day's assigned reading as a group. It was only after he had encouraged our active and vivid participation in this way, by literally coming down to our level, that he might share key points of literary analysis, always interweaving them with our own contributions and comments.

Of course, the words of Thoreau, Ralph Emerson, Annie Dillard, and Barry Lopez were so powerful that there was not much left to add or say. We took in the majestic words, and each student in the class interpreted them based on personal experiences. And that seemed to be precisely our professor's point: that literature evoked something different in each of us. The very fact that these works ushered forward, in each of us, unique reflections and powerful emotions was the measure of the authors' success.

In our class of twenty-three students, Professor Sanders created magic, giving us immersive learning without ever leaving the classroom. And it was such fun. Unlike the discomfort I experienced while facing down gender discrimination in Susan Gubar's class the previous semester, Imagining Nature brought me joy and became my favorite classroom hours every week. Nature was something I knew, loved, and cherished, and somehow our indoor class felt like outdoor exploration. Class was like an academic story time, with Prof. Sanders as our thoughtful guide. Our inclusive discussions meant that we came to know each other well. I started sitting with an insightful classmate, Julie, who became a lifelong friend. I venture to guess that our course and our professor ranked as the most memorable academic experience for not only me but also my entire group of classmates.

My fondness for Professor Sanders and his course is the reason why, when the Little 500 track opened up in early February, I started coming to class in full cycling gear, with a notebook and pen in my cycling messenger bag slung over one shoulder. That way, I would not miss a single lesson. I could ride straight from class to the track for our practice. I felt that I could miss neither a moment of that class nor a moment of practice time on the track. The track hours were limited to two hours daily, and we were committed to being there for as many hours as we could manage with our course schedules.

I was a little self-conscious the first time I strode into class at Ballantine Hall decked out in cycling attire from head to toe, with my helmet dangling from my bag. Given the familial vibe Scott Sanders had created, I should have known that the others would simply ask the backstory, as my family members might if I came to the dinner table wearing a mask. After all, Professor Sanders had stimulated in all of us the appreciation of a story, the fine art of telling it well, and the connection with one another. I shared my story, what I knew of the race and my participation in it, with my classmates.

The first week the track was open was reserved for Rookie Rider Week. The veteran riders were not allowed on the track for that first week in order to allow ample time for new riders to partake in drills, instruction, and training with members of the Riders' Council, who were experienced upperclassmen committed to helping ensure the races' success. All newbies had to complete several Rookie Rider Clinics and also a mandatory minimum number of hours practicing at the track, where it was required that you sign in and out each day. Being that it was the first year of the women's race, we were all rookies—that is, first-year riders in the race. So the track was bustling.

The addition of the women's race that year meant that women and men alternated the early and late track hours each day, which made the track a busy place with literally hundreds of cyclists needing to get their practices in. Scheduling the Rookie Rider Days helped avoid mass chaos in the first weeks of open track. Although some informational meetings had been held in the first semester, we had really only seen some videos of the men's races that explained the basics of the race. There had been the skills workshop on how to do bike exchanges in Dunn Meadow. But from a look around later, it did not appear as if *anyone* from *any* team except the Thetas had mastered bike exchanges.

The Little 500 track was in the Bill Armstrong Stadium, located on the outskirts of campus, near the IU Memorial Stadium, the football field, and Assembly Hall, the basketball arena. It sat above, up a wooded little entrance road across from those facilities. During the fall semester, it was the home of the IU soccer team, whose home playing field was on the infield of the track. The soccer team was using the adjacent practice fields most days during our spring semester, even though it was their off-season. The IU men's soccer coach, Jerry Yeagley, had created a powerhouse soccer team, which would go on to win the 1988 national championship the following fall. (It would not be Coach Yeagley's first but rather his third national championship, putting him in Knight's league, but he was still no match for ole Doc Counsilman's six titles.)

In support of the strong soccer program, Bill Armstrong Stadium had undergone a renovation a few years earlier, which included a new grass surface on the playing field. Yeagley was thus not too thrilled that the Little 500 track, which formed a large oval around the soccer field, brought hundreds of students who might (and did, I assure you) trespass on the expensive and carefully maintained grass surface. He and his staff issued continual reminders and more than a few grumpy (but surely warranted) shouts, to Little 500 riders: *(Please) do not step or walk on the grass!*

Stepping onto the Little 500 track for the first time was an exciting moment. The Armstrong Stadium seemed bigger than I remembered from my attendance at an IU soccer game months earlier. We had imagined how it might be to ride on the surface made of black cinder. Now we would finally be able to experience the shifting cinder under the wheels of our track bikes. But not yet. First, we had a bunch of information to take in. Hand signals that we should use, track etiquette that might save you from getting hit by someone sprinting or coming out for an exchange. Where to find the first aid table if you fell and got scraped up or, worse yet, black cinder ground into your wounds. Where (designated outer lane) and what the rules were for making exchanges. What the stoplights meant. Yes, stoplights. The big oval track had small stoplights in each of the four corners, and the lights gave information about the conditions on the track. Green light meant smooth sailing. If there had been a crash, the riders were "neutralized" with a yellow light, meaning slow down and proceed with caution. That one became a factor on race day. The red light, well, I don't need to explain that one.

Amy looked at me as we listened to instructions for how to properly move within the pack. "Slower riders have the responsibility to move toward the outside of the track to allow faster riders to pass using the inner lane," the veteran riders explained.

Amy whispered, "Sheesh! This is crazy!" She raised her eyebrows and flashed me a smile. Then she added, "We're just gonna have to be faster than everyone so we don't have to ride in the pack." Kristin heard her too and laughed.

If you thought about it for a minute, just one sane minute, Amy was absolutely right. Little 500 *is* crazy. I mean, amazing, yes. But really and truly? A bunch of college kids racing heavy single-speed bikes around an unbanked cinder track, doing these awesome (a fine exchange being true fluidity of motion!) but (let's admit it) silly exchanges to keep the team's momentum moving even as they switched riders? Sounds like a recipe for disaster. The whole concept is a bit whacked if you think about it for a moment. So, from then on, I didn't.

When we were finally set free to ride our first laps, everyone was polite and riding very respectfully, at least for the first day or two. The clinic was led by the Riders' Council, consisting of the Theta riders and some other women who had raced in the Series' events during the previous year or were involved with helping organize the whole event and a few of the men's Riders' Council members who didn't really do much. It seemed deliberately designed to put a scare into us rookie riders. And well, I guess that was probably the correct approach. If you didn't follow the rules of the track, bad things could and likely would happen. See my earlier comments—the whole concept really was a recipe for potential mishaps. When we were cut loose to ride, everyone was very carefully riding the oval, signaling, and calling out their every move.

"Yip-yip-yipee . . . Let the fun begin!" I shouted to my teammates as I finally headed out of our pit and rode my first laps. The track felt great. The cinder was relatively hard-packed, and it felt more stable than the gravel-like feel I had expected. What I did not expect was how much fun riding in a circle could be and how much it could inspire speed. I yelped out a spontaneous "Woohoo" as I flew past our pit after that first lap, trying to remember all of the rules about passing other riders.

It was time to see how riding the track was at high speed. "On your inside!" I called out to riders as I passed them on the left, taking the innermost lane next to the slightly recessed sloping cement gutter. I was so psyched to finally be on the track that I could not resist sprinting across what would eventually be the finish line, at the halfway point of the front straightaway. Kirsten had hopped on our other bike. She joined me for the next lap, and we sprinted against each other across the line, coming in almost dead even. I threw my arms high in the air to celebrate the victory over her, despite being uncertain whether I had actually beaten her.

The Roadmaster bicycles that had been issued to each team were not high-tech dream bikes, but they were not as clunky as I had expected. The bikes were, in fact, the opposite of high tech, created by the same brand that made the low-cost bikes available at Kmart and ShopKo, the Walmarts of the day. That, of course, was a financial consideration so the race would be accessible to all. You could change almost all the parts on the bike, although the rules indicated precisely which replacements were allowed.

The Little 500 *Manual*, referred to as the bible by some, gave the parts' specifications, rider eligibility rules, rules of conduct for racers and coaches alike, and race regulations—in such exacting detail that it was about fifty single-spaced pages, no kidding! Kevin had returned from a meeting a few months earlier with one hefty copy of it and told us we were all supposed to read it. He shook his head back and forth, saying, "I didn't know what I was getting into! Look at this thing. I am not sure any of us knew what we were getting into. Girls, this race is serious. Don't fight over who gets to read this first!" He laughed and tossed it on the table.

Kirsten picked it up, opened it to a random page, and said, "OK, here we go: 'Illegal recruitment is defined as making cash payments or giving other perks to riders for their services.' Jeez, we aren't riding in the Olympics here, people. But, actually, maybe I can make some money next year. Or perks. What kind of perks are they talking about?"

She flipped a few pages and read, "'Rookie riders must have achieved a minimum 2.0 GPA in the fall semester.' Uh-oh, anyone out?"

Louise responded, smiling, "No, but it's a good thing I dropped that chemistry class or I might have been."

Kirsten continued, "OK, listen up. The penalties section: 'One. Failure to observe flags, two seconds. Two. Creeping will not be tolerated. Track position and relative distance to the leader must be maintained during caution conditions signified by the yellow flag.' Tucker, you got that?" Kirsten said to Amy, accusingly. "No moving up on the sly when the yellow's out!"

Amy balked, "Wait. Why are you telling me? I'm no cheater! I win fair and square."

By the end of that first practice, I was exhilarated from endorphins, effort, and excitement. The track was surprisingly smooth and faster than I expected. Within a week or so, I would come to realize that the cinder surface could break down a bit and become like kitty litter, especially when we followed a men's practice with full attendance. Then, you might feel a little slide or shift, and it was easy to understand how that could freak out riders with less experience or less confidence on the bike, which defined basically everyone in the women's race.

I could see why Little 500 was famous for its crashes and pileups. I had heard that part of the fun of watching the race was watching breakaway attempts, but the biggest crowd-pleaser was a crash. Let's face it, for much of the college-aged crowd, the big pile-on crashes provided definite entertainment value. Kind of like the fights in hockey games. I once read that the vast majority of hockey fans like the brawls and actually oppose a fighting ban. Same thing with crashes. Sad fact about humans: we love watching misfortune and violence.

Our Willkie men's team also consisted of all rookies since they were all first-year students. Kevin was doing double time as coach of both. Each team had been issued two official Little 500 bicycles, the only bikes you could use on the track. Since we had the two teams, we Willkie riders actually had four bikes. Often the guys left us their bikes after their track time ended and vice versa on the days we practiced first. That way, we could have four bikes at a time on the track, instead of just two. Only two riders from each team could be actively riding on the track at any time, but it was still really helpful to have three or four bikes so that you could practice two-bike exchanges and have different size track bikes available. A few other dorm teams and some women's teams had extra bikes like us. We liked having four bikes even if it was a bit of effort to coordinate passing all four bikes back and forth every day between the men's and women's teams.

It didn't always work out perfectly, and often I was going back from the track to our dorm riding one bicycle and hauling along another with my free hand. I learned that if you grabbed the stem of the extra bike, right in the middle of the handlebars, bringing a second bike back was not too hard. Except for climbing the hill. Just as the dogs played a role in helping our sprints, struggling up the Fee Lane hill past McNutt Quadrangle with an extra track bike—and mind you, the track bikes were not light carbon-fiber or aluminum frames—helped my strength and handling skills as much as any targeted practice. McNutt, closest to the football stadium, was the party dorm in those days, and sometimes I would hear a random shout come my way from a dorm room window as I worked my two bikes up the hill.

Anyway, that first day the guys practiced after us, so they started showing up in the last ten minutes of our practice. Euphoric and slap-happy after our introduction to track riding, we bantered with them about the fun they were about to experience.

I summed up what they'd experience in the next two hours: "First, they're going to scare you out of your minds telling you about crashing, telling you how the cinders dig into your skin so deeply that they have to scrub them out with a steel brush in the ER. Then when they finally let you do some riding, you have half the group going super-cautiously slow while the other half is just loving the track and flying. Honestly, kind of a dangerous combo. And definitely ironic after the whole discussion. So, yeah, have fun!"

"Wow. Can't wait. Thanks for the preview," said Rob.

I smiled and admitted, "Actually, no. Seriously, it's a real blast. Just take the inside line." I offered to ride Rob's bike back to the dorm in order to leave them the track bike. It turned out to be the perfect size for me. When I ran into him at dinner a few hours later, he told me that the addition of testosterone to the mix made their practice total chaos.

"Thanks for the tip, but I didn't take the inside. Didn't seem too smart," he told me.

"Glad you used your own little thinking cap then," I told him.

"Hey," he said, "about going out for that dinner together. What are you doing Friday?" And just like that I had a date with a nice college guy. I smiled inside and out.

We survived Rookie Rider Week with flying colors. We had even started to get our exchanges down. I was taller and Kirsten shorter than the others, so we decided to use two bikes in the race. That meant that we had to do two-bike exchanges, a special hybrid of the regular (one-bike) exchanges. When we came zooming in for a two-bike exchange, our teammate would be waiting at the start of our exchange zone. The incoming rider would tag her as she flew by, and the outgoing rider would then sprint, leap on her bike, and be off. The job of the incoming rider was more complicated. The bike had to come to a full stop by the end of our pit, marked by a white chalk line. Not wanting to sacrifice any speed when it was me coming in, after the tag I would jam on the coaster brake hard, skidding in, and then jump off the bike and stop my body by the line. To stop the bike, I would lift it off the ground, and it would swing out over the pit line (only surpassing the line in the air) as I whipped it back on the other side of my body. We were determined to make sure that the team lost no more time in the two-bike exchanges than in regular exchanges. We worked hard to perfect them.

I had often trailed behind my younger sister Molly with my technical skills in sports such as soccer and swimming, but these exchanges felt natural to me just as being on a bicycle in general did. It was as if the bike was just an extension of my own body that I controlled innately. I had always been a natural on the bike. We became adept at the two-bike exchanges quickly. I concentrated my efforts and proudly mastered them. Other coaches sent over their riders to learn by watching us.

Willkie Sprint on race day. From left: Kristin, Kirsten, Amy, Kerry, Louise, and Kevin. *Photo courtesy of Kristin McArdle Ryan.*

In the 1950s, the only opportunity for women to race on bicycles was the Little Little 500, in which women from sororities competed in a relay race, exchanging the bicycle while passing an egg on a spoon.
Photo courtesy of Indiana University Archives.

Participant in the Mini 500 trike race at a packed Assembly Hall.
Photo courtesy of Indiana University Archives.

Rob and Kerry in 1988. *Photo courtesy of author.*

Wearing their newly minted T-shirts on the day of Quals, Willkie Sprint poses for the team photo to appear in the official Little 500 race program. *Photo courtesy of Indiana University Archives.*

Team Willkie Sprint lined up and waiting for the starting gun of the Team Pursuit finals. *Photo courtesy of author.*

Rob and Kerry. *Photo courtesy of author.*

Around lap 4, the pack is still together. Kerry is in the front row, in the
yellow jersey with the rolled sleeves. Officials display the yellow flags.
Photo courtesy of Indiana University Archives.

The pack passing pit 8 in the first laps of the race.
Photo courtesy of Kevin Wentz.

Shot taken early in race. Kerry is in the center breathing hard. *Photo courtesy of Indiana University Archives, scanned from* Halls of Residence *publication, 1988.*

A bike exchange in action: Kerry is stepping off the right side and passing off to Louise. *Photo courtesy of Kevin Wentz.*

Nerves in pit 8: Amy (in helmet) warms up on the trainer, while Kristin bites her nails behind. *Photo courtesy of Indiana University Archives; copyright WTTV4.*

High anxiety: wild gestures and shouting at Kirsten as the team fears that she will be caught in lap 98 and freaks out accordingly. *Photo courtesy of Indiana University Archives; copyright WTTV4.*

Celebration erupts in pit 8 as Kirsten crosses the line.
Photo courtesy of Indiana University Archives; copyright WTTV4.

The team cheers as Kirsten arrives in the pit after crossing the finish line.
Photo courtesy of Indiana University Archives.

Swarming Kirsten in a celebration hug.
Photo courtesy of Indiana University Archives.

Kirsten's perfunctory coach water dump. Kerry's sister Ann looks on.
Photo courtesy of Indiana University Archives.

The trophy presentation by Bill Armstrong, for whom the stadium is named. *Photo courtesy of Indiana University Archives.*

Podium shot. *Photo courtesy of Indiana University Archives.*

Willkie Sprint meets with IU President Thomas Ehrlich and his wife, Ellen, on the infield before the men's race. *Photo courtesy of Indiana University Archives; copyright WTTV4.*

Silliness with freshly painted helmets in the Willkie bike room, dressed and ready for the team banquet. *Photo courtesy of author.*

Team selfie at IU's Sample Gates on their return in 2023.
Photo courtesy of Kristin Ryan McArdle.

CHAPTER

MY ROOMMATE, KAREN, had joined our dorm's Mini 500 team. She would participate in the race on an oversized trike, the only option that had been available to women previous to this year. Aside from being a vestige of the sexist and seemingly outrageous past in which women had been relegated to a far inferior experience, the trike race was a whole lot of fun for those who competed in it. The teams had trikes issued to them and practice times, meeting over in Assembly Hall on the basketball court in the months leading up to the race weekend.

For whatever reason, we stored the Willkie team's giant trike in our room. It had, like all trikes, one gear, and the challenge was to get your legs absolutely churning. It was hard for us to resist the call of the giant toy. Plus, we had that long L-shaped dorm floor hallway. Cindy, Louise, Karen, and I would pull it out for some afternoon or evening fun and just get it raging fast down those long straightaways. A passenger could stand on the ledge over the rear axle; so two people could barrel around on it. Our RA Crys was also on the trike team. She did not approve of our antics but could only shut down the dangerous fun if she was present on the floor. She was a committed and vigilant RA. It was likely only thanks to her near-constant presence curbing our tricycle romps that we never injured anyone while flying down the dorm floor at warp speed.

Tired of dorm food, but also of having anyone at all as an authority figure (although Crys was certainly kind and helpful that year), Karen and I decided to live in off-campus housing the following year. Her friend Tara from Cincinnati was also studying at IU, a few years further along than we were. Tara was already renting a five-bedroom house in a perfect location close to campus and the iconic Kirkwood Avenue at the heart of student life, and we were able to put our dibs on two rooms that would be vacated by graduating seniors. In late February, Tara invited us to a house party there to get a taste of life at our future home on the corner of Eighth and Dunn Streets.

That same night, Rob and I had our dinner date. He stopped by Willkie North to pick me up. He exited from the elevator on the eleventh floor just as Karen and I whizzed by on the trike. He took a turn on the trike as well, and then we headed out—but only after asking Crys, who exited the elevator we entered, whether we could participate in *both* Little 500 and Mini 500. She said no, but only because the Willkie trike team had no space for additional riders.

Rob and I walked through campus and out through the Sample Gates, which separated campus from the city, feeding us out right in the heart of downtown. We continued up the hopping Kirkwood Avenue, with its bars and restaurants already filling, to the picturesque downtown square featuring the Monroe County Courthouse. Just across Sixth Street we found Leslie's Italian Villa and the table for two Rob had reserved. The restaurant was quaint and cozy, but it was not actually a villa. Leslie's was located in a historic limestone building with "Princess Theatre" printed in faded block letters across the facade.

We were feeling very adult and tried to order glasses of wine. The idea fizzled when our waitress asked for our identification. We were both sort of baby-faced and clearly younger than Indiana's legal drinking age of twenty-one. I didn't mind as I did not drink much of anything alcoholic really. During weekend partying, I might have a beer, a mysterious party brew, or a shot of hard alcohol in company. I had not acquired a taste, though, for any of these. Along with my baby face, I had what my brothers called a "baby tongue," meaning I usually winced when the alcohol hit it.

First-date energy filled the air. I told Rob about seeing Sting play a few nights earlier at Assembly Hall, a stop on his Nothing Like the Sun tour. Rob had been there too. The crowd had chanted "Roxanne" all concert long, begging until Sting finally conceded and played the famous Police song. I had gone with Karen but looked around the packed Assembly Hall for my friend Roxanne, who had a love-hate connection with that song.

Then our conversation turned to the teams—his, which it seemed would be fighting to qualify for a spot in Little 500, and mine, about which he oozed, "You guys could win this thing!" We talked about our families, discovering that we both had four siblings (his were all brothers); the joy of action-packed households; and our hometowns. Rob hailed from Morton, Illinois, a small village that was the "Pumpkin Capital of the World." We discussed our classes and what we would declare as our majors the next year. He planned to enroll in the B-School, which is how students referred to IU's School of Business. He also wanted to study economics. And political science. "I am thinking maybe I'll get two bachelor's degrees, a bachelor of science and a bachelor of arts," he said.

"Oh, that's all," I said, smiling at his ambition. He said he would choose it all if he could. I could relate to that.

I was unsure about what major to choose. During my first semester, I had taken The Solar System A100 and loved it. I was thinking about becoming an astronomy major since I had always been so fascinated by stargazing. My professor had been excited that I was interested and told me to take calculus, which I was enrolled in. It was going well, but I was starting to think I might not want to focus my life so much on what was going on outside our planet when there was so much I loved about the happenings on Earth. The other option I was considering was English. I liked reading the classics, and I was a decent writer.

Rob said, "You're hired. Next paper I write is coming your way before I turn it in."

"Deal," I responded, thinking he was obviously more organized than I was. A world-class procrastinator, no matter how I tried to convince myself to change my ways, I usually finished my papers at around 3:00 a.m. on the day they were due. And that was the handwritten version. I also did not type and hired my friend Roxanne to type them for me. Since she wanted the cash for what she called "party funds," and she knew I was a procrastinating night owl, Rox told me that I could bring the papers at any hour of the day or night. I would head over to her place at whatever hour of the night. There I would find her wide-awake and waiting.

Rox had what looked like an electric typewriter, since the very first personal computers had bulky keyboards in that shape. In the mid-1980s, hardly anyone had personal computers in their homes. We called them "word processors" since that was all they really did for you in the pre-internet days. I had finished college before someone invented the World Wide Web, and it only became available widely years after that. Rox's setup was something we might put in a museum now. It was the Apple II Plus, one of the first personal computers developed by Steve Jobs. Rox had it connected to a dot matrix printer. And let me tell you, that printer was loud. Luckily, she had her own room, but I was surprised she did not wake up the entire floor when the printer went into action. Once I chose to become an English major, I paid her a fortune before finally taking a typing class one summer.

I told Rob about the one-credit elective course that Karen and I had enrolled in together that semester. Modern Dance had been Karen's idea. She thought it might be fun, and I thought I might finally learn a few moves. Our teacher, Clive, was a graduate student who seemed to be much older, maybe in his late twenties. He told us he was from Ohio, but he had what sounded a lot like a British accent. Clive's movements seemed to be an extension of his words. He did indeed have some moves that I unfortunately never learned. He ran the class by playing music that inspired the particular movement techniques he would be teaching that day. The class, not too surprisingly, had an entirely female enrollment. Karen was right in there with the others, but I seemed to be the least graceful of the group. This frustrated our teacher to no end, but it cracked up Karen and me in equal measure. Our classroom in the Performing Arts Department had a full-length mirror on one wall. As Clive demonstrated the move of the day, we watched and replicated his motion. Karen and I planted ourselves in the rear, but there was no hiding with the mirror reflecting my awkward, stiffly athletic attempts to match Clive's flowy gracefulness. He would leave the class members to practice and walk around correcting us. Karen would generally burst out laughing when Clive made the usual beeline straight for me.

Our grade for Modern Dance was to be determined by a performance in pairs to a particular song. Karen and I had chosen Pink Floyd's "Time." Earlier that day during class, I recounted to Rob, Clive could not take it anymore as he watched Karen and me practicing. Previously he had been very encouraging, as though his gentle nudging would bring about a breakthrough and I would finally get it. This time, he came over and corrected my movement as usual. But then in frustration, Clive burst out, "OK, so you have got to try to relax your muscles! Look, you're clearly very athletic, and you have these beautiful long legs, dancer's legs, these long arms . . . You are . . . *your body is made for these movements*, but . . ." Flustered, Clive seemed unable to put his sentiment in words. "If *only* you can *relax* and *flow*." He stopped himself there, but that was enough. I had flushed red in embarrassment at Clive's comments. I understood his frustration stemmed from the fact that while I had the long limbs, strength, and the tall thin frame that is usually the ideal dancer's body, I just was not wired for modern dance—at all. Rob laughed heartily at the retelling, just as Karen and I had on our walk back to Willkie after class.

Rob was interesting and interested, articulate and fun. As far as I was concerned, dinner alone would have sealed the deal. But we had the house party next. We left Leslie's Italian Villa, drunk from attraction rather than wine, and walked the few blocks to the house party. It turned out to be raging. We heard the music pumping from up the block, and I was happy to see my future home could host a rocking *festa*. *Good to know*, I thought, although I am not sure why because I did not party much anyway. Tara saw us enter from across the crowded room and made her way over. She smiled widely, and as she nodded her head to the beat of the music, I could see that she was happy about the party's robust turnout.

When Karen showed up with some of our friends, including Cindy and Louise, Tara gave us all a tour of the house. "You guys are going to love living here," she shouted over the music. I sized up the potential rooms, dreaming of landing the one room that was spacious with big windows but paying little attention to the tiny shoebox-sized room that would actually become mine the following fall. The four upstairs bedrooms shared one small bathroom with an antiquated clawfoot tub that looked a little dingy inside. The house was objectively in pretty rough shape overall. In other words, it was a typical student rental. But compared to our dorm room directly across from the RA, it seemed like heaven on earth. We returned downstairs, and Tara showed us the keg of beer and the wine-with-floating-fruit concoction she called Powdy Punch. Who could resist the allure of the magic punch with the inviting fruit floaters? As I sipped mine, I guessed why it might be called "Powdy": one serving likely left you slurring and unable to properly pronounce "party."

Rob and I settled in the dining room, where the music was deafening but still somewhat less so than in the living room with its large set of wooden tower speakers and people tightly packed against one another like sardines. The floor vibrated along to the thumping bass, the partygoers dancing, or maybe both. The windows were open to let out the heat from the crowded room and sweating dancers, and the cold February air felt refreshing. Rob and I sat on the sills of the two large dining room windows. Unable to hear one another, we ducked our heads out of our respective windows to meet on the outdoor side, where we could have at least some minimal conversation over the din of Prince's "Let's Go Crazy." We denied it when Karen came over and accused us of going on the other side of the glass to smooch. "We just can't hear anything in here," I claimed, but actually the smooch did sound like a good idea.

"Especially since her voice seems to go up ten octaves with every sip of her drink," Rob said, as he gestured to me. It was true. I did not have a whole lot of experience with drinking at the ripe old age of eighteen, but there seemed to be a direct correlation between how much I drank and how high-pitched my voice became. The more I drank, the more I started to sound like a six-year-old. Go figure. And at that point, I was sounding pretty darn squeaky and childlike.

We had our own little Willkie contingent at the party, all of us feeling fortunate to have been invited to a house party. Under the drinking age, bars were off-limits for those like me who had no fake ID. And the dorms had a no-alcohol policy unless all persons in the room were twenty-one or older. Of course, that never happened because no one was still living in the dorms when they reached age twenty-one. We hung out for a few hours at the party—drinking, dancing, and well, shouting out a few lines of conversation. At one point, I heard Karen saying, "Listen, you've got these long legs" in her version of Clive's accent. She was replaying my humiliation in dance class that morning, as I had earlier. Given what Clive had said, Cindy was convinced the teacher was hitting on me, but Karen assured her that Clive did not seem the type to hit on a female.

I jumped up and made an announcement: Karen and I would be performing. We gave a rousing performance of our Modern Dance routine, the one we had been creating for class. I knew that Tara and her roommates would have Pink Floyd's *Dark Side of the Moon* album. We had choreographed our performance to a song on that album, "Time." The raucous party quieted down for a moment as we cued up our song. It started with us on the floor in yoga's *balasana* pose, also known as the fetal position. I stared down at the carpet and made a decision: I vowed that we would get a new rug for the living room first thing in the fall. *Gross.*

At some point after the much-heralded performance by Karen and me, Rob and I made a move for the door. As we headed off on the cold night, we were warm and buzzing with the energy that comes with the combination of drinking, loud music, dancing, and laughing. It was already a date night success, but it was not over yet. We walked across Dunn Meadow, chatting excitedly. Friendship and the spark of something more glowed between us. As we got closer to our side of campus, we slowed, seeking a way to keep the night going.

We found it. As we passed the Delta Gamma Sorority house and took a shortcut through the woods behind Read Quadrangle, we came upon some abandoned-seeming old buildings. "What are these anyway?" I asked, as they appeared out of place on our carefully maintained campus. They were sort of hidden in the woody area above the creek that ambled through campus, so I had never really noticed them. We found them open and walked in to discover that they were being used as art studios, maybe for graduate students in the fine arts program? We could not find a light switch, and it was hard to see much of anything. We found what seemed to be a big pedestal to sit on. With our feet still planted on the cold cement floor, we lay back, side by side on the pedestal, and continued chatting. We continued our half-drunken half-falling-in-love conversation, occasionally breaking for passionate kisses and clumsy hugs in our big winter jackets. For who knows how long, we alternated back and forth between the two. Finally, cold and coated with dust, we left the studio, which we christened with the name the "Love Shack"; headed back to our dorm; and bid farewell with a hug and high five. I entered my room quietly to find that Karen was already in bed with the lights off. From the darkness, her voice rang out, "Hey, seems like that went well!" I agreed that my night with Rob had indeed gone really well, and I told her about the Love Shack.

We slept in until 10 a.m. and awoke only because there was someone knocking on the door. "Jeezus, who is waking us up on Saturday morning?" said Karen as she got up and cracked open the door.

"Shit," I said from up in my loft bed when I saw Kirsten in the doorway, fully dressed in cycling clothes and ready for our ride. *Our ride!* She came in, and Karen returned to her bed.

"Good morning, sunshines!" Kirsten called out cheerily, entering the room. It was not too often that I found anyone's cheerfulness irritating, but her voice triggered a pounding in my head.

"I forgot. Our ride!" I felt like there was a thick mass of cobwebs in my head where my brain should have been. Opening my eyes, the brightness, daylight—all these things hurt.

"I gotta say, it smells like a brewery in here, ladies," Kirsten continued. "Did we have fun last night?"

"Headache" was my response and also my attempt to get her to lower the levels of both her voice and cheeriness.

I considered whether I should bail on the bike ride or climb down from my loft and suit up in my cycling gear. My bed felt like the right place for me, in that moment and in the near future. But I knew that Kirsten would keep on until I got up. So I did.

"Fine. Give me five minutes," I said, padding off down the hallway to the bathroom. The fluorescent lights in the bathroom buzzed in a way that I found particularly annoying. I had never noticed it before, so clearly it was related to my headache. As the details of the previous evening flooded back to me though, the pain in my frontal lobe was lifted by some measure of my happiness from the night before returning as well. I did not understand how my body could literally warm while thinking of the freezing Love Shack.

Once we were out on our bikes, Kirsten rode next to me, telling me about her nutrition class and what she was learning. She was always so *awake* in the morning. "We have got to focus now. I think we should get on the athlete's diet." At first, I thought it was her way of scolding me for my hangover. But she went on and on. She told me about the effects of sugar and alcohol and how she had stopped eating meat.

"Did you know that they are going to pass a law requiring all food packages to list nutrition facts on them? People need to *know* that stuff," she continued, "because how else is the average person supposed to know what all this sugar and these cheap oils are doing to us? That's why Americans are getting fat." I had not realized that Americans were getting fat, but Kirsten seemed pretty alarmed by it all.

"Well, they have all the 'light' versions of stuff now," I offered.

"Yeah, but it's half lies," she informed me with disgust, "and totally useless information. What good is the light version if it's worse for you because of fake sweeteners that, get this, *are known to* cause cancer in lab mice? Anyway, when they started spelling it L-I-T-E, everyone should have realized what a sham that stuff is. 'Lite' stands for artificial. It's in the name."

We had the whole team out together, and we stopped for a pee break at Riddle Point Park on Lake Lemon. Kirsten rattled off something about good fat versus bad fat and filled us in on what foods were key for cyclists. I loved nothing better than a homemade chocolate chip cookie, full of butter, sugar, and fat, so I was sad to hear Kirsten condemn them for being full of bad fat. But with the fog of my headache starting to lift, Kirsten's claims about the evils of alcohol, fat, sugar, and the like seemed valid. She definitely thought changing our diets was important to harnessing the maximum from our physical efforts. I guess it made sense. When Kirsten suggested that we cut the "junk" out of our diet, we all agreed to it.

"Sorry to interrupt about the food stuff, but . . . can we please, please take the route that avoids the three-legged dog?" Louise asked, unable to focus on anything but our vicinity to the dog we all feared. We agreed in unison to take the slightly longer route that did not go by the dog we called Pirate, who overcompensated for his gimpy three-legged gait by barreling after anyone who passed in an impressive show of barking, drooling, and teeth-baring fierceness. Louise, in particular, was terrified of Pirate.

"No sugar and no alcohol," Louise said slowly, playing the idea out in her head now that her terror at the thought of passing Pirate had subsided.

"I am not giving up my ranch dressing though," Amy chimed in.

"Yes, you are," shot back Kirsten, "and I am giving up my Cool Ranch Doritos, too."

"Me...want...cookie," I said in a sad baby voice as I twisted my fist near my eye, playacting a baby wiping away tears.

"Well, I think it's a good idea," Kristin said. "I am in. We all should be." And that was that. We made a pact to eat like champions for the next seven weeks until race day. Despite my sadness about cutting out cookies, I was thinking it might be pretty cool to see if it improved our performance.

We bid farewell to Lake Lemon (as well as sugar, alcohol, and fat) and hopped back on our bikes. As we headed back toward Bloomington, we straightened out in a long paceline, rotating through short pulls at the front to help each other through the significant headwind. A U-Haul truck passed but was moving only slightly faster than we were. I was at the front and jumped behind it to get relief from the strong wind. Kristin was behind me and followed.

"This is awesome!" Kristin shouted about the wind block that we were getting in the truck's slipstream. She shifted left, and we formed two lines, taking full advantage of the draft from the truck. As the truck accelerated a bit, so did we, determined to hold on to our free ride in the wind pocket created by the truck. For me, that moment conjured up the scene in the film *Breaking Away* where the main character drafts behind a Cinzano semitruck until he triumphantly reaches the speed of 50 miles per hour, thus earning a salute and honk of the horn from the truck's driver. The driver did not clock us, and we did not last too long in the truck's draft. But feeling inspired by our own effort, I let out a yelp, "Woo hoooo," which was followed in turn by a litany of whooping from my teammates.

CHAPTER

EVERYTHING STARTED HEATING UP with the start of March. We were practicing for hours each day, including daily time on the track and long weekend rides to keep our fitness up. The track practices were both fun and intense. There was a lot to learn and perfect. We practiced exchanges until they consistently went smoothly. Kevin worked on figuring out who made the best combinations for exchanges. Should I pass off to Kirsten or Louise? Which incoming riders were best suited for fast exchanges with each of us? Since we were doing two-bike exchanges, what order of riders would be most efficient? Kevin showed up at the track daily with a clipboard and began taking our splits as we did exchanges and clocking us doing laps. As we rode lap after lap, Kevin tried to figure out who would be our endurance riders and who would be our sprinters. He relished solving the puzzle of our relative strengths and weaknesses and determining our best strategy.

Endurance on the track translated to being able to ride hard for a longer period of time without getting exhausted, while sprinting involved being fastest in high-intensity moments. While I had solid endurance capabilities, Amy and Kirsten could sprint like nobody's business. That meant I might ride more total laps of the race, staying on the bike for longer pulls. It would make no sense, however, to have me on the bike at the end of the race if it came down to a sprint. Our speedy sprinters would better handle a sprint to the finish. Kristin and Louise fell somewhere in between. Neither of them was fond of making exchanges, and both had taken a bad fall or two and skinned their knees.

There are not many sports in which you practice right alongside your adversaries. One aspect that made the Little 500 special and such a fun intramural sport was the social component during the long afternoon track sessions. By early March, the track was open to rookies and veterans alike. My teammates and I were there daily, maybe coming in late or leaving early if we had a class but always managing to fit in an hour at the track. Since the women's race was entirely new with no veterans to serve as guides for the others, we were all in the dark and feeling our way through the process of preparing for it. Each team was required to have a coach, and some teams had found coaches with experience from the men's race, either as coaches or athletes.

Kevin took his job as coach seriously, especially since he saw that we women had the potential to do well on race day. He was also coaching the men's team, an uphill battle with all rookies. Being on the track for their practices as well as ours allowed him to observe the way experienced teams practiced. Unfortunately, he could also see the difficulty for Rob, Joe, and the other guys, competing against guys who had been training for this race for years and came in much better prepared as a result. Rob and his teammates recognized it too.

While Rob and Joe remained committed to training, the other riders resigned themselves to a poor result and practiced half-heartedly, if they even showed up at all. I felt bad for Rob, but he was OK with their fate either way. Rob was pretty academic, and his focus was on getting good grades in the rigorous business school. He was doing Little 500 just to have something else going on outside of studying.

Often Rob and Joe remained to watch some of our practice, or we, theirs. We spent a lot of beautiful sunny spring afternoons riding our bikes in circles at the track, going nowhere and everywhere all at once.

Rob and I often met after dinner and went off together to study. We usually chose Woodburn Hall's quaint library with cut glass windows, the Fine Arts Library in the spectacular triangular modern Museum of Art built by famous architect I. M. Pei, or the comfort of the big red couches at the Memorial Union's various student lounges. We alternated studying with long breaks involving exploration of every corner of campus.

On one such study break, I told Rob all about Sunday Lake. I was working on a paper for Scott Sanders's class, one in which I had to describe a powerful experience in nature. How could I use words to convey its magic, as Sanders had done in describing his own childhood? Professor Sanders was an established writer, as we had discovered by reading a carefully worded essay in which he described his childhood years, growing up on a munitions plant. I wanted to describe Sunday Lake as vividly as Sanders had painted his stomping grounds and their effect on his worldview. "This poison I also carry in my bones, this conviction that we build our lives in mine fields," he had written, conveying so much in so few words. I was trying to describe my experience of nature at Sunday Lake, and I read my draft to Rob to get his opinion.

I sometimes listened to my Walkman as I studied. Rob had made me a mixtape of jazz music including Miles Davis and David Sanborn. I did not like the music much. Given the platform of rock music I listened to, I am not sure why the honking of the trumpet and saxophone seemed too aggressive and abrasive to my ears. Nonetheless, I did like that he wanted to share it with me. I gave Rob *The Little Prince,* a slim book by Antoine de Saint-Exupéry in which the narrator encounters a child prince who has left his very small planet, Asteroid B-612, needing a break from his beloved but demanding rose. I was not sure I understood the lesson that the author intended to convey in the simple yet nuanced story. But I loved the world he created, the little prince, and his fragile rose. Rob, in turn, gave me *Jonathan Livingston Seagull* by Richard Bach. It was a story about a seagull who dared to be different than the rest of his flock. We would sometimes take our study breaks without going anywhere. Rather, we would stretch out for some reading time, abandoning the Union's wooden study tables for its plush red leather couches. Coming of age ourselves, Rob and I found meaning in the little prince's loving acceptance of his rose, no matter how fragile, and in Jonathan Livingston Seagull's bold and free-spirited pursuit of his unique potential.

"*Grazie per il libro; è molto figo*," I told Rob, using the Italian slang I had learned that week from my Italian teacher. (Thanks for the book; it's very cool.) That semester, I was taking Elementary Italian. There was a four-semester foreign language requirement, and I had chosen Italian to celebrate my liberation from the usual suspects of high school language acquisition—Spanish, French, German, and of course, Latin, which I had taken for four years in high school.

My dad had weighed in on my choice, telling me, or at least making sure I understood, that Italian was only spoken in one country in the world.

"Even French is spoken in a few dozen countries . . . but Italian? Do you even know anything about Italy, hon?" I did not, or at least not much anyway. I was just excited to have a new choice.

"*Basta*," (Enough) I told him, "*ho già deciso*—I've already made up my mind." My Italian teacher was a graduate student who had just spent a year in Florence. She had a style of dress that was entirely foreign to me. Rob had taken years of Spanish and could understand the gist of my meaning when I spoke to him in Italian, which I did but only with accuracy in the limited situations that fit my knowledge. That did not get me far. I could comment on the weather, introduce myself, ask how it was going, and that was about it. However, the limitations of my knowledge of Italian did not stop me from making up the rest.

"*Che cazzo stai facendo?*" (What the @%$*# are you doing?) I shouted to a rider who swerved and cut me off at the track, remembering the Italian slang that I had learned from my two New Jersey classmates. After a week or two of sizing up our competition during track practice, we discerned that we ranked within the top ten teams, maybe even the top five. The Theta team appeared to be, by far, the fastest and smoothest in those opening weeks. There were a handful of other strong individual riders to watch out for too, but not too many teams had a lot of depth.

Each team arriving at the track chose the pit out of which to base their practice that day. The pit gave the two off-the-bike riders and the coach a place to hang out and space to stick the extra bikes. Because of Kristin's friendship with the Thetas, we often set up our practice pit near them on the track, at the start of the back straightaway.

The Thetas were the only women's team in their second year of preparing for the race. They had retained the same coach who had coached them the previous year when they attempted to qualify for the men's race. A longtime coach of the Acacia fraternity team, their coach loved and seemed to live for the Little 500, driving down on the weekends from the Chicago suburb where he lived to coach his teams. Impassioned and opinionated, he was sometimes a controversial figure. He stood out for being more experienced and much older (in the ripe old decade of his thirties) than the other coaches, who were generally students themselves like Kevin. The status of the Thetas' coach had been cemented when he had been given the opportunity to play the bit part of coach in the movie *Breaking Away*. Positioning ourselves next to the Thetas, Kevin and the rest of us learned by osmosis. Of course, the whole lot of us riders had learned exchanges from the Thetas. We all knew their story. They were the heirs apparent to the women's race. No one actually expected to beat them with the race six weeks away. Except maybe Kevin.

None of that stopped us from dreaming about it. There was a jovial atmosphere at the track, maybe even more so that first year as we all confronted the steep learning curve together. Our own ambitions combined with that atmosphere of conviviality to produce a fun, competitive banter between us and the other strong teams in those weeks leading up to the race. In respect to the Theta team, underneath the words was a bit of a mutual admiration society. We had awe and respect for them because of their courage and drive to bring the women's race to life. And I think they recognized, through us and our excitement, the very evidence that what they had done was worth it. We stepped onto campus as freshmen and had, thanks to them, the opportunity to compete in an organized race that would give shape to our college experience. Anyone could see that the Theta riders enjoyed being at the track, maybe in part just to marvel at the amazing response to what they had created.

"We need a name," said Kevin as he and Kristin started up our meeting. Rob and I sat together on the couch of the Mason Hall lounge, where all our teammates had gathered to hear about the series of pre–Little 500 races that were about to begin. "Kristin and I have a few ideas, but you guys need to play a role. Obviously, we need to include 'Willkie' in the name. But then we can add whatever we want."

"So it could be the Willkie Speed Demons or the Willkie Cheetahs or whatever," Kristin added. "Anyone have ideas?"

"Not the Cheetahs; it would just make me hungry for something Kirsten won't let me eat. I love Cheetos," said Amy, smiling. As I nodded in agreement, she added: "I kind of liked Wes's team name, the Posers, because it's funny."

"Yeah, but it's too negative," Louise weighed in. "We have to choose something positive."

"Anyway," piped up Joe with a smile, "'Posers' might describe us, the guys' team. You girls, though, you are not posers; you're the ones that the others are trying to pose like! You guys should be more like . . . Willkie Dominatrix?" Everyone laughed.

"Ha ha. Not happening!" I said, turned off by the sexual connotation. "Anyway, we are not dominating anything for now."

"Unless it's the number of visits to the medical tent or the amount of cinder that will scar my knees for life. That's the only record that I am setting, y'all," said Louise, who was having a tough time getting her exchanges down that week. She was sick and tired of scraping up her knees falling on the cinders. So was Kristin.

"Yeah, Louise and I are doing well there—both gonna be marked for life," added Kristin with a laugh. We had heard a rumor that any cinders that remained in your wounds would be there forever, small dark cinder "tattoos" that attested to your participation in the Little 500. That was the reason the folks in the medical tent took a steel wool scrub brush to your new wounds in an effort to remove all the black cinders.

"Seriously, I am going to get us all kneepads!" I said. "For the team name, I think we need something short, like one syllable, since we already have 'Willkie' in there," I continued. "Willkie Speed?"

"Well, one of our ideas," interjected Kevin, "was Willkie Sprint. What do you think about that?"

"Pretty much sums it up, I guess," said Kirsten. "Sprinting is what we're going to be doing, hopefully faster than anybody else. So my idea of Willkie Psychos just lost out to that."

We agreed, and Kevin officially registered us as Willkie Sprint. With the small budget that she had managed to secure from the dorm, Kristin ordered us some red winter riding jackets with the team name printed on them, just in time for the first event of the brand-new Little 500 Series races. That year, the IU Student Foundation had decided to expand beyond the World's Greatest College Weekend and offer an entire month full of new racing events leading up to race day. It all started that weekend with the Prologue on Friday afternoon and the Team Time Trial on Saturday.

The Prologue was an individual, two-mile effort up North Jordan Extension, a sort of fraternity row, and back. It was required that all Little 500 riders compete in some, but not all, of the series events, so there was a healthy turnout—over a hundred men and eighty-four women. Only Amy, Kirsten, and I signed up from our team. Kevin could not make it to the race. Wes came with a trainer so we could warm up right near the start line. He brought jelly beans with him and told us of champions who swore by sugar pills to stimulate their adrenaline before racing. With our new commitment to eating well, we declined the jelly beans. But when Wes then offered them to some of the other women standing around waiting for their start time, we got mad at him.

"Wes!" I admonished, "Why would you help our competition?"

"Come on," we cried.

"Well, I have a huge bag of these. I gotta get rid of them so I don't eat them myself" was his only defense. He grinned and shrugged his shoulders.

"I am on the verge of diarrhea from being so nervous," said Kirsten. "The last thing I need is a bunch of jelly beans."

When I finally lined up for my turn, I too felt almost nauseated from nervousness. It was the first competition after months of training. We were using our personal bicycles, not track bikes, since this was a street race. I had been worried about choosing the best starting gear so I had pedaled up the hill slowly a few times, trying to figure out what would work well for the slightly uphill start. Unfortunately, I chose poorly. I felt instantly distressed as I struggled in a gear that was too difficult to turn the pedals over easily and give me a good starting speed. I downshifted and jammed on the pedals, rocking my bike back and forth in my effort to make up any seconds lost due to my poor gear choice.

College kids take any excuse to party, and we provided one that Friday afternoon. The road had been closed off, and the residents of the Greek houses had come outside to watch the race. Entire fraternities and sororities were out on their front lawns kicking off their weekend partying and screaming encouragement as riders passed one by one. I reached the first fraternity, and as I passed, a cheer emanated from the pack of students standing on the road-side drinking from plastic cups. A few fraternities had kegs of beer on their front lawns and music pumping. These spectators were an extra motivation for me to make a strong effort. I figured that they, in particular, would be the type of fans to definitely let me know if I looked like an idiot. By the time I reached the turnaround, my legs were burning and my throat felt scraped raw from breathing in the cool air. On my way back, I spotted Kirsten racing up, and her intense expression got me to dig a bit deeper myself. As usual, I fed off her intensity.

Jelly beans or not, we ended up placing well. Amy took second place, I took fourth, and Kirsten sixth. Amy was interviewed and quoted in the student newspaper. She said that we had done the race for extra training and to see how we stacked up against the others. We were encouraged by our results, but we also noticed that some of the stronger riders had not competed in the race. We were left wondering how we would have stacked up had they also been there.

The next day, we were to race in the Team Time Trial, a ten-mile out-and-back race in the Morgan-Monroe State Forest. We were nervous. Tears had been shed when we had gone out a week earlier to the stretch of road where the race would be held to try a practice run. The TTT involved riding in a paceline, smoothly exchanging the role of pulling the others by blocking the wind at the front. For all of us, racing in a pack was a new skill, as was pacelining. Each team's final time for the race was determined by the moment the last of their four riders passed the finish line. So it made sense to ride in the paceline, each taking turns pulling at the front, and to finish together. In our practice run, we had each fried ourselves while pulling at the front and subsequently had difficulty hopping back on to the wind-protected rear of the paceline. There was a lot of screaming, as each rider reentering at the rear after making a big effort at the front struggled to get back in the slipstream.

"Wait!" Kirsten screamed when Louise was unable to catch back up. Then when Kirsten herself struggled to get back on, she again shouted, "Wait!" Apparently we did not.

I am not sure whether no one heard her or no one listened. I had heard something undiscernible but had not really taken the energy away from the physical effort at hand to ask her to repeat it. Mistake. Man, she was not happy watching us ride away. When Kirsten finally did make it back on, her temper flared. "Goddammit! 'Wait' means 'wait'! What good does it do us if one rider is back there alone? It's the fourth rider whose time counts." She was right, of course. It was a team effort, not an individual one.

Kevin was in a car following behind us, and he flagged us to a stop where the turnaround would be. Bungled by our inability to maintain a steady speed, our attempt had been disastrous by any measure but even more so by our perfectionist standards. Our strengths and weaknesses were amplified and more evident over that longer distance.

Sullen, Louise said, with exasperation, "I'm just not fast enough. I might as well just stay at the back the whole time. Actually, no, behind Kerry—it's like a rope tow," she said, referring to the generous slipstream created because I sat so tall on the bike compared to our shorter teammates. "But I can't even do that! I can't do it." She was near tears.

"I can't either!" Kirsten, red-faced, was having a bad day. "I don't know what's wrong with me," she raged. "I just don't know. But jeezus, it doesn't help for you guys to ride away."

Amy, Kristin, and I, silent until then, all started in at once. "Sorry . . ." "I didn't know if I should slow or stay with the wheel in front of me . . ." "I thought that I heard you but . . ."

"OK, everyone just hold on a second," said Kevin. "*Relax.* Everyone just relax." He told us our split was not bad and that we were a bit disorganized in our paceline—he could see that from the car following behind—but that "it was not tragedy level."

"Kirsten, do you remember what you told me when I puked outside the Schwinn shop?" I asked her, before then reminding her: "Are we maybe just taking this a little too seriously? Here's the thing: we came to that first meeting just wanting to do this for fun, just to have an activity to meet some friends and get involved."

Kristin broke in. "I wanted our dorm to have a team, that's all. I never imagined that we would happen upon you guys, all freshmen and full of talent. You might not know that I am studying sports management. I dream of working at the Olympics someday. So just like Kevin, no one forced me to be here because I am an RA and someone had to do it. Working with you guys has turned out to be so much fun and even perfect practice for my future. You have all picked up this sport and learned it in a few months. And your drive

. . . Each of you is so motivated. I am really inspired by you guys. But if we want to come together as a team, we have to do just that—come *together*, as a *team*. Just imagine what we can do if we can pull together, unite our efforts, and ride as one smooth, well-oiled machine where everyone has different but equally important roles.

"Here's what I am going to do, for our team," Kristin continued. "You guys know that we can only suit up four riders on race day, right? All five of us have been training hard, but only *four* of us can ride in the race. Well, it's going to be the four of you. I just think that it'd be cool for you guys to ride it together as an all-freshmen team. I think that you are good enough to make the podium, maybe even win. I am going to keep riding and training with you. But I also . . . Kevin and I spoke about this. I am going to help with coaching from here on out too. We are going forward together. But on race day, *you four* are going to represent us on the bikes. And you have to unify to do it well. Think as a team. It's our only shot at being our best on race day. So, let's get back on our bikes and work together for the next five-mile stretch and prove that we can do this, that we can synchronize with each other, compensate for who's having an off day, and ride this thing together—as a team."

We stood in stunned silence. We knew that only four could ride on race day but had never spoken about who would not. Not once. Kristin had founded this team and now she was offering to step aside, to give up her spot. Louise immediately reproached her: "*No*, no way. Kristin, you should ride."

But Kristin immediately interrupted, saying firmly, "This is already decided. I'm not going anywhere. I'll still be riding with you all. Now let's finish our practice and get on with it!" And so we did. With Kristin's words fresh in our heads, we focused on riding that paceline as one. But I was also thinking about her news and how selfless she was.

Standing on the start line for the Team Time Trial a few days later, with both Kristin and Kevin present and giving us encouragement before we set off, I thought back to that moment. After Kristin's words, we had managed to smooth out our paceline on the five-mile stretch back toward the start/finish line. We had ridden it in as a team, which is all we needed to do on race day. They called our team to the line. Cyclists and coaches, we all put our hands in for a collective cheer, calling out "Team Willkie Sprint!"

We took off like scared animals when the gun went off, sprinted up to speed and then regrouped. In our new Willkie Sprint team jackets, we formed a streak of red snaking down the forest road, struggling to stay simultaneously together and at our fastest possible speed. As we sliced through the wind together, it seemed that the carrot we were chasing was not staying in the draft or winning the race but rather being a generous teammate and kind friend. There was still some shouting, but no tears were shed. We placed third in the Team Time Trial that day and were satisfied with our effort. The Little 500 Series was off to a great start for Team Willkie Sprint.

Once the race was over, Amy and I wanted to tack on some extra miles, so we decided to ride home the long way from Morgan-Monroe State Forest after our Team Time Trial.

"Hey Tucker, let's swing by and visit Pirate's place," I said. "We can see if we still have enough in our legs to outsprint him after that race. Besides, it's the most scenic route back." We still could not believe that a three-legged dog was so fast. Fierce little Pirate gave us a run for our money every time. We quickly settled into a side-by-side chatting pace as we headed off on the rolling roads that would take us past Pirate's home and back to Bloomington.

"Hey, that looks like my house," said Amy, pointing as we rolled past a trailer home. Assuming that she was kidding (but also learning, in the same moment, never to make assumptions), I burst into a hearty laugh.

"Well actually, I'm serious," she said, matter-of-factly, "but it *is* pretty funny."

I did not breathe for a moment. *Wait, what? What did I just do?* I wanted to die right then.

"Open mouth. Insert foot," I said out loud, and in my head, *Why? Why did I laugh? I am such a jerk!* "Sorry, Amy. Ooh God, I'm so sorry. I didn't mean to laugh at your . . . I didn't think . . ." Suddenly I seemed unable to complete a sentence. I tried again. "I mean . . . I thought you were kidding."

Amy let out a howl with laughter. "Yeah, I got that," she said. "You obviously didn't think I was serious. Don't worry about it. I don't care. I was just sayin' that looked just like my house. 'Cause it does."

"OK," I said, silent a beat. "But still, I feel bad!" Boy did I.

As we rode in, she told me about her family: her dad, whose metabolism she had inherited but whom she had not seen much after her parents split up, even though they lived in the same town; her mom, a cosmetologist who had pretty much spoiled her rotten to make up for her parents being divorced;

and her brother, who had been caught in between. "My mom's probably my best friend," Amy added. "She'd do anything for me."

"My mom's like that too," I responded. "She's my number one fan."

Pirate seemed to have missed us—we had been doing fewer road rides—and he charged at us with more vim and vigor than ever. We sprinted until we wore him out, or was it that he wore us out? I got to thinking about how dogs and drunks were similar. Mostly they were happy, but the mean ones could turn you off to the whole species.

We arrived in Bloomington and caught a red light on Tenth Street. It was another opportunity to practice our "track stand," the position on the bicycle where you stand on your pedals, balancing rather than unclipping from them while waiting for the green light. We balanced there, moving slightly forward and back. Suddenly, feeling a little unstable, I reached for my brake. In a flash I was down, lying on the street, still clipped into my pedals. Amy was asking if I was OK and trying not to laugh when she went down too. Embarrassed and shaking with peals of laughter, we got back up quickly and dusted each other off before waiting for the next green light, each with one foot solidly on the ground.

"Hey," I shouted to Amy as we neared the point where we'd each separate to head for our respective warm showers, "you know that I couldn't care less about whether you grew up in a mansion or a trailer home, right?"

"You still worried about that?" was her response.

"Yeah," I said. I was. "You know I love you just as much no matter where you came from, right? Because I do."

"Yeah, I know that," she answered. And we headed our separate ways.

CHAPTER

AT THE TRACK, we heard that some of the sorority teams were heading on spring break trips. It was common practice for the fraternity teams. Teams able to do so got a nice break from the Indiana rain and could enjoy riding in warm temperatures. A bonus was practicing exchanges on sandy beaches with soft landings instead of cinders. Our team did not have the resources to go anywhere. The budget that Kristin had secured from the dorm had covered the jackets, some new bike parts, and some other smaller expenses, but it was nearly gone.

Chatting on the phone with my brother PJ, I griped about being stuck in Bloomington while everyone headed off on spring break. Five years older than me, PJ was just getting going on a career as a professional poker player. He was essentially living out of a hotel in Vegas, where his winnings easily covered his expenses.

"Bummer, Kake," he said, using a family nickname for me. "Well, why don't I fly you to Vegas, and you can hang out here for spring break?"

"Really?" I said. I had only been to Las Vegas once as an eight-year-old, traveling with my parents and sister Molly on a driving trip. At the time, we had spent a miserable day driving through the desert coming from San Francisco. Death Valley in August earns its name. My parents had made the mistake of hauling us through that 110-degree desert at high noon with no water and in a car with no air conditioning. Such Wisconsinites. Molly and I had frantically rolled down the windows of our newish VW Rabbit.

"But Dad, it's just hot air! It's worse than before," Molly said.

"Yeah, it feels like a hair dryer!" I chimed in. Molly and I were convinced that we would die.

"Look!" My mom pointed to the first view of Vegas, with its colorful lights, appearing in the distance.

"It's like a mirage of foolishness," she said, not very subtly tipping her hand regarding her feelings about Las Vegas and gambling in general. Why, we asked, would they have built this city in the middle of the desert? This was long before my parents had to shift their perception of Las Vegas due to their son becoming a professional poker player. They would be forced to have a reckoning about Vegas and gaming, but it would come some years later. On that driving trip in 1976, my parents had no connection whatsoever to the strange city in the desert. We had only come because Dad had a conference there. My parents "donated" some money to our hotel, the MGM Grand, playing slot machines as my sister and I watched from the line on the floor, past which minors were not allowed.

"There is nothing to do with kids in this dirty place," said my mom, stuck entertaining my sister and me while Dad was busy with his conference. When she took us to Circus Circus, an entertainment venue featuring more carnival games and rides than we'd ever seen in one place, Molly and I begged to differ. While she mumbled about the prices, we had the time of our lives. Mom was happy to be leaving as we drove out of town a few days later.

"Well, girls, say goodbye to Las Vegas, the city of sin," she said. I watched as the blinking lights of the Strip receded. As we passed by a string of colorful wedding chapels, I tried to understand what was so sinful.

Consistent with a lifelong campaign to prove that Mom and Dad were not always right about everything, my brother convinced me that Vegas was actually not bad and that we would have a blast going to shows. His was a generous (and my only) spring break offer, and it definitely beat going home to Wisconsin weather or staying a week in the dorms with no one around. Anyway, PJ had started to whittle out a living playing poker and I was curious.

"I will probably win the entire cost of your flight and room here at the Stardust in a few hands of Texas Hold'em, Kake. So don't worry about it. I have got this covered." Essentially he was a total success in my eyes, just by being able to offer me a free spring break spent in a hotel on the Las Vegas Strip. He flew my sister Ann out from Madison for the same week, and the two of us stayed in a room together. At age eighteen, I was too young to gamble, but Ann had just turned twenty-one. PJ gave her a few hundred dollars to play the slot machines.

I was instantly able to see what PJ was building. He had sent a limousine to pick me up at the airport. When I arrived at the hotel, there he was, twenty-three years old—although he had always looked younger than his age and was still barely even growing facial hair—sitting at a poker table full of middle-aged men. PJ was stacking up a mountain of poker chips on the table in front of him. The leaderboard on the wall above his head listed him as the poker room chip leader.

A year earlier, when he had told me that he was going to become a millionaire by age twenty-five, I had wanted to believe him. He has always worn his brash confidence on his sleeve, and I had been schooled in enough family games by him to take his premonition at full face value, no matter how worried my parents were about him dropping out of college. In Vegas, he took us to eat at the finest restaurants, where he often tipped an amount equivalent to the price of the entire meal. Money seemed to have lost its value to him. He seemed to have no worries about it arriving steadily. We went to a different spectacular Vegas show every night. He lavishly spoiled Ann and me. I also saw that he was really good at poker, and, aside from whatever else that meant, it affirmed my faith in him beyond the typical adoration of a younger sibling. I had witnessed the recent years in which my parents struggled to accept and support his chosen vocation, and it had been hard to decipher whether their concerns were valid. Those days in Vegas renewed his status as a rockstar of a brother.

While Ann played slots every day, I headed off to the Las Vegas Athletic Club. There, I rode the fitness bike like a madwoman and worked out like crazy. I took my brother's rental car out to Red Rock Canyon a few mornings and hiked up to the top. Then I rented a bike for a few days to do some road riding too. In the afternoons, my sis and I enjoyed laying out in the hot desert sun and shopped—PJ had given me a hundred dollars, which was a boon for a starving college student in the 1980s.

"I am Siegfried" and "I am Roy," announced the stars of the long-standing top-selling Vegas magic show involving white tigers and white lions. My brother was connected enough to get us some front-row seats to amazing Vegas shows. *Siegfried and Roy* was the top show in town. Their full-grown wildcats were enormous, and with no barriers between us and them, the front-row seating was a true thrill. I had no doubt that we were safe but did wonder how they had received permission to parade these giant wild animals merely ten feet from us.

"Oh my God!" Ann screamed on impulse as a tiger took a step forward and roared directly at us. She grabbed my arm. PJ and I chuckled. But I also understood her fear when, a few minutes later, the tiger gazing our way licked its chops. Thrilled with our front-row seats, I realized too that we were closest to the wild tiger.

Another shock for a midwestern kid was the amount of nudity on display when we attended Stardust's own show, *Lido de Paris*. Neither my sister nor I was prepared for the hour-plus-long parade of topless showgirls. My brother had warned us that there would be topless dancers. But I did not expect them to be the main feature of the show. The show seemed to be essentially focused on their nakedness. My albeit-limited life experience told me that these "showgirls" with caked-on makeup and their breasts flying in the air were being exploited to provide some cheap thrills for men. To me, their high kicks and jazzy dance moves seemed like an elaborate attempt to sell sexualized cheerleading as an upscale Broadway show. Probably due to my midwestern and feminist roots, eight years of Catholic schooling, and the nudity shock factor, the show seemed to me to be a throwback to a different era. My assessment at the end of the show could be summed up by the word *cheesy.* I did not agree with my brother that the show was world-class, and in the end, we could only agree to disagree.

"You have the best tan on campus," Rob told me a few days later, after I was back to reality in Bloomington.

"Yeah, I invested an hour per day in the desert sun out there," I said, "but I have been freezing ever since I got back. I am from Wisconsin and all, but I am pretty sure my body wants me to live in warm places." We were at the track, and the Bloomington sun did not match the heat I had quickly become accustomed to on spring break.

We had one week until Little 500 Qualifications, which would determine our pit positions on race day. Kevin and Kristin got busy taking our splits as they tried shuffling the rider order. The idea was to see whether changing the order in which we rode made any difference in how quickly we managed to finish the four laps, riding one each. Two days before Quals, we turned in our bikes for the IUSF mechanics to check over and certify that all of our parts met the regulations.

"I can't believe that they are so worried about people cheating," I said, wondering if the IUSF policy of having mechanics check the bikes over with a fine-tooth comb was really necessary.

"Well, that's because you maybe don't understand yet how coveted winning Little 500 is on this campus," said Kevin.

"Yeah? Is it *that* big a deal? Isn't it just a little bit excessive, having a fifty-page rule book and making all these checks?" I shook my head. But Kevin and Kristin, the only ones who had actually been to a Little 500 race, exchanged knowing looks with one another.

"I know. It's hard to imagine a college intramural race is such a big deal," Kristin said, "but . . . well, you'll see." Kristin, rather than Louise, was riding Quals with us. Although she had decided to defer to the four of us freshmen on Little 500 race day, we had decided as a team to alternate riders throughout the Little 500 Series races.

Thirty-one teams raced in the women's first Little 500 Qualifications. There was no possibility of not qualifying for the race. That is because the total number of women's teams was fewer than the limit of thirty-three teams that could qualify for race day. We were still nervous about Quals though, because this race had an effect on the setup for Little 500 race day. The Quals' winner won the "pole position," the same term used to describe the pre-race leader in the Indy 500 car race. Their prize was being the first to choose the pit where their team would be located on race day, followed by the second-place team and so on. The pits were laid out on both straightaways of the oval-shaped track. Some pits were better than others because they were easier to approach coming out of the turns or less congested with surrounding teams doing their own exchanges. If we could do well in Quals, we would be able to lock up one of the most favorable pits for race day. We also wanted to position ourselves near the Thetas, to keep track of them as we expected them to be the race leaders.

The Thetas went early in the day and set a smoking hot time of 2:41 for the four-lap Quals relay. When our turn came, Amy started us off with a blazing pace. She came in and exchanged the bike with Kirsten, who kept up the hot pace, but then came in a bit too fast for the exchange with Kristin. The bike ended up flying off solo, with no rider. Kristin chased after it, picked it up and continued. She exchanged the bike with me after her lap, and we intentionally did a very slow exchange to be sure not to bungle it. I tried my best to get up to speed quickly and save our attempt. However, our time was way off. Since we had three possible attempts, we opted to make a second attempt after finishing that round poorly. Unfortunately, the next two attempts also went poorly and we finished in eighth place. Our high hopes had been dashed by the reality of slow, unsightly exchanges. We were deflated.

"I guess that we aren't as good as we thought after all," said Kirsten.

"We just have to be better at our exchanges," said Kristin. "If you think about it, we still got eighth and our exchanges were sucky. Think if we had good ones."

"Yeah," said Amy, "if we had nailed our exchanges, we'd definitely be like fourth or fifth, maybe even second or third."

"Now wait a minute, Amy," said Kevin, "if you nailed your exchanges, there's a chance you could have even won. Don't think the Thetas are unbeatable. They hit all their exchanges perfectly today. Absolutely perfectly. That's all. You guys are right in there with them other than that." I wanted to believe Kevin, but I wasn't sure.

"Kev, the Thetas' time was 2:41 today," I said. "Two minutes and forty-one seconds. Then two other teams got 2:45, and the next team, the fourth-place team, finished in 2:51, ten seconds down from them, *ten seconds*. Out of under three minutes. That's a ton! One, two, three, four, five, six, seven, eight, nine, ten. If you think about that much time being lost in four laps, think how much we could lose on them in one hundred laps. We were thirteen seconds slower." I frowned.

"Don't go down that path," Kevin said to us, "of expecting everything to go well for them on race day and poorly for us. So they had a great day today. So we had a rotten day. The results show that. So what? Don't read anything else into it. We don't do an exchange every lap on race day."

"And honestly," said Kristin, "our exchanges are usually some of the *best*. Just not today. You were nervous. You've all started to really care more about this race, so you were nervous."

"It is true that we usually have good exchanges," Kirsten agreed. "I don't know what was wrong with us today. I haven't fallen on exchanges like that ever."

"Now you know how it feels," said Kristin, with a smile, "and you won't let it happen again, I bet."

"You know what?" asked Kevin. "I think that it's almost good that you all screwed up today. You got your nervousness out today. Today we had a rotten day. We aren't going to have a rotten day on race day. I really believe that."

The worst news that day was not our own frustrating result. Rob and his Willkie Sprint men's team had failed to qualify for the men's race. They had somewhat anticipated that possibility, and while Rob and Joe had continued to practice, they had done so essentially solo, without other team members present. Joe and Rob were both visibly crushed. But since there is no use crying over spilt milk, they joked about it.

"The pride of Willkie Sprint rests in your hands," Rob told us as we left the stadium.

"Thanks, Rob," said Louise. "No pressure or anything."

Several days later, Kristin and Kevin went to the official meeting to pick our pit and jersey color. Kevin was set on selecting a pit in the back straight-away, maybe the second or third pit after you exit from the turn, thus avoiding both the need to cut out of the turn too tightly on the exchange laps and the confluence of many teams on both sides. Choosing eighth, he did not expect to have his wish granted. In a stroke of luck, other coaches apparently did not agree with his strategy and we landed a pit not far out of the turn. The bonus was that we would also be close to the Thetas, who chose the first pit out of the corner.

Next, Kevin and Kristin got to choose our jersey color. We were waiting for their return after the meeting, and upon seeing us, Kristin asked, "Now tell me again what color you wanted?" Given her question, I wondered excitedly, *Did we get the yellow? Why else would she ask?* Earlier, we had discussed the colors we all preferred, and yellow was our number one. We assumed it would be everyone's first choice. After all, yellow was the color of the famous jersey worn by the cyclist leading the Tour de France. How could it have been available after seven other teams chose?

"Yellow? Come on, don't tell me it was still available," said Kirsten.

Louise widened her eyes and smiled, asking, "We got the yellow jersey?" To which Kristin, having successfully created her moment of suspense, finally nodded emphatically up and down. The news about the jersey and pit was just what we needed to get over our disappointment with our eighth-place Quals performance.

"We're in yellow? Yes!" I yelped, throwing both arms up above my head as if I had won something big. "So we got everything we wanted? This is an omen," I said, hopping up and looking toward the heavens with my hands fashioned in a prayer.

"Maybe it is," said Kevin, glancing skyward himself. "But keep your feet on the ground. We are turning the page now. We have Miss-N-Out this weekend, Team Pursuit next weekend, and then the Little 500 race obviously is the week after that. So not much time. I need you girls to focus now."

Each team had the responsibility of painting the large wooden pit boards that went behind our team on race day with a design that had to be pre-approved by the IUSF. Kristin was organizing the entire project with our support crew, a group including our friends and some of the upperclassmen RAs who served as our supporters behind the scenes. Their proposed pit board design cheerily announced "Willkie Sprint" in large cursive script and "World's Greatest College Weekend" below that. The colorful script stood out on the bright white background spackled with drops of color. Once Kristin had our design approved, she proposed that we make a bunch of T-shirts using a similar design.

"We can use the money from selling them for race day supplies or a big dinner out together the night before the race," she told us.

"Yes to the dinner out," said Amy, always hungry. "Good idea, for sure."

"I think we should put 'No sugar. No fat.' on the back of the T-shirt," said Louise dryly. She was not a huge fan of our self-imposed diet. And I had to admit, up on the eleventh floor of Willkie North, we had struggled to stop ordering late-night breadsticks and garlic butter. That delightful combination from Pizza Express was a true hit on our floor. It fueled lots of fun and definitely some weight gain (the freshman 15) too.

"OK, you guys laugh now," responded Kirsten, a die-hard believer in our dietary restrictions, "but you should be thanking me, and you *will* be thanking me. I can't believe the abuse I take for trying to get you all healthy."

"Yeah, well, apparently you are way ahead of your time because the members of Willkie Sprint are the only ones holding back on the garlic butter," I said. "But hey, even if it's a painful loss, I am willing to take that hit for the team," I added with a fake stoicism.

"Actually, maybe we should have the big dinner *after* the race so we can order whatever we want to eat," said Kristin with a chuckle.

"I do have some breaking news," said Kirsten. "I started eating meat again. I told my nutrition class professor that I basically had no energy. When I told her about how much I was training, she told me to go right out and eat a burger. Or two. She was like, 'Go straight to McDonald's because you need protein to grow muscle.' So yeah, that's what was wrong. You guys feel better knowing I failed on my own nutritional advice?"

"No," I said, "of course I don't feel better that you had no energy. But I am pretty much a vegetarian, and I feel fine." It was true. My mom had become a vegetarian two years earlier, and our family had gone from literally buying half a cow to store in the basement freezer to eating lots of quiche and fettuccine alfredo. "You sure you need the meat? Did you tell her you were working too?" I asked.

"Maybe," I said, suggesting the obvious, "just maybe, you are doing a bit much, girl?"

In response, Kirsten explained that she already felt way better eating meat again.

"Then you might feel even better if you go full hog," I said. "Ice cream has protein and calories—a triple-scoop cone might be the answer to what ails you." Maybe I was merciless, but Kirsten had been so self-righteous about the nutrition stuff, I had to needle her.

"You guys won't give it up, will you?" she said.

We all shook our heads back and forth in unison, and I, for one, held back a laugh. Nope.

"No, Kirsten," said Amy, "you kinda brought this one upon yourself by taking away my ranch dressing."

Our Willkie dorm mates had seen us coming and going on road and track bikes all year. We had established Willkie Sprint as a contender in the women's race and a source of pride for our dorm. We were convinced that we would sell a lot of T-shirts to our dorm mates, who would surely want to wear them to cheer for us (in large numbers) at the race. Or so we thought. We went big on quantity when placing the T-shirt order. Unfortunately, it turned out that the tees did not exactly sell like hotcakes. In the end, we might have exaggerated the degree of pride our fellow Willkie residents had in us.

As we studied one evening, Rob said to me, "It turns out that our little T-shirt sale is like a lesson from the B-School textbook regarding supply and demand. Supply is there. Demand? Not so much." We had to keep lowering the price to try to sell the Willkie Sprint T-shirts and still ended up with half a box of them in the bike room.

"You know," I said, trying to think like a businessperson, "*Ascolta*. Listen. I think we have failed in the marketing of the product. Take you, for example: you haven't bought enough! Just one for yourself? That's it? When you . . . You're always thinking about IU presents to buy for your family, and you have all those brothers who would look great in Team Sprint tees . . . We definitely missed the mark on the marketing campaign."

That Thursday night, Kevin and Kristin organized a team showing of *Breaking Away* at Mason Hall. Our women's team plus Joe and Rob showed up. We all crowded into the dorm room where Kevin and Kristin had the TV set up and the popcorn waiting. We settled in and watched the story unfold on the campus and country roads that had hosted our own story of the past few months. We vowed to ride out and find the limestone quarries in the film. We were a lively crowd and cheered loudly for the Cutters, the ragtag group of townies who took on the preppy college fraternity team. The story was very relatable for us. We were somehow a bit like the Cutters, being the scrappy underdogs ourselves, both on the bike and off. We were inspired by the Cutters' glory.

We laughed hard at the scene where the main character, Dave Stohler, allows a customer to return a lemon car to his father's used car lot. In disbelief, his father gets upset, tries to physically push the car back off the lot, and suffers a heart attack while chanting, "Refund? Refund?" The roles of father and son were particularly well played and surely contributed to the film winning the Oscar.

"I love that character, Dave," I said at the end as the team sat together in the glowing post-movie moment of conversation.

"That's because you *are* that character," Kirsten responded. "Going around everywhere on your bike, always all happy about everything." She chuckled, but somehow it had not really come out like a compliment.

"Well, yeah. What's wrong with being happy?" I asked, guessing that it was being so happy that was the noncomplimentary part of Dave Stohler, and maybe me too.

"I can just tell you got lots of hugs growing up or something," Kirsten said. "I'm probably just jealous. That's all."

"Nothing's wrong with it," Kristin jumped in. "I got lots of hugs too. Everybody's different. Anyway, let that movie inspire you guys for next week." Kristin was keeping quite busy coordinating our inspiration on many levels—from making T-shirts to assisting Kevin with coaching us to painting pit boards to soliciting funds to cover our expenses.

After the meeting, Rob came up to my room. Karen was off studying, and we hung out chatting for a while.

"You know, Kirsten's right. About you and Dave Stohler being alike. And she doesn't even know you are taking Italian. Add that to your similarities. Anyway, I love the way you are happy from the time you wake up in the morning," Rob told me. "*É molto bello.*" Aside from having unsinkable positivity, the Dave character was obsessed with all things Italian—learning the language and even renaming the family cat "Fellini."

"Speaking of *molto bello*, I have that classical music from the movie stuck in my head now. It was perfect for all the cycling scenes," I said. "I think it's Mendelssohn. Or maybe Johann Sebastian Bach. My parents are totally into classical music. I was raised on the stuff. In our house, National Public Radio is playing like 24/7."

The next day, the music-loving (and information-seeking) Rob reported back on the symphony. He had looked into it, especially since he loved studying at the music school and likely had been there that day. Remember it was pre-Google era. Searching for information was a physical act.

"OK, so you were right," Rob said. "It was Mendelssohn's Symphony number 4 in A major in the movie. Opus 9 or something. Felix Mendelssohn was German, and I guess he wrote that after his first trip to Italy, which he said was like the 'supreme joy' of his life. It's called the Italian Symphony. He wanted it to be his happiest piece and his most 'sportive.' That part that you like, the first movement, he wrote it to represent the sunshine and warmth of the Italian countryside." Well, that explained why I liked it.

"Wow, cool, prof," I said. The guy really did like learning. I imagined that Rob had been happy to have an excuse to go check out the resources about Mendelssohn at the IU Music School. To my surprise (why here in Indiana, I wondered), the Music School was ranked as one of the top music schools in the world. Rob had discovered that you could study at the hallway tables outside the practice rooms in the Music Annex. There, you could catch talented student musicians perfecting their playing in what felt like a live concert.

A friend from Madison who played the French horn, Anne, had come to study at the IU Music School a year earlier. She eventually spent four years in those practice rooms; graduated; went on to the other top music school, Julliard; and then ended up playing in the Metropolitan Opera Orchestra, where she's been ever since. She and I used to drive back and forth together on holidays. Her parents lived about six houses down from mine on Madison's Lake Mendota lakefront. Once, she gave me a lift home from Indiana on a visit that she had not announced in advance to her parents. She wanted to surprise them. We often left late to avoid traffic on the long segment of our journey home that passed through the heavily congested Chicago area. That night, we arrived in Madison at two in the morning. She had devised the plan, on our way up, to announce herself by playing the French horn in her parents' backyard. Despite the cold winter wind off the lake trying to foil her plan by blowing her musical notes away immediately as they exited the horn, she persisted. I was awed by the beautiful sounds that she produced in her snow-covered backyard. Eventually, a light went on in an upper bedroom and then another. Curtains were pushed back. Anne would have elicited emotion in anyone who heard those few notes she played on her French horn that night, so beautiful was her playing. I could only imagine her parents' rejoicing in her early return.

That beauty and emotion were available to anyone who discovered the tables outside the practice rooms in the Music Annex—albeit mixed in with lots of droopy notes and practice scales. I think we were the only ones aside from music students who did. We added the Music Annex to our favorite study spots. The circular building had apparently created perfect acoustics in its practice rooms by constructing each of them with one concave and one convex wall. I was glad that Rob's love of exploring every corner of campus led to the discovery, allowing us to experience the special and amazing musicians of the IU Music School.

"Italian countryside, Indiana countryside—not quite the same thing, I guess," I said. "But that Mendelssohn symphony? It was in my head all day. I doubt I will have that music playing in my head tomorrow in the race." I was hoping I might be relaxed enough the next day to hear classical music replaying in my mind as I raced.

The Little 500 Series continued during the final two weekends before race day and included the final two events. The next day, we had the individual event called Miss-N-Out, and the following Saturday, a team effort called Team Pursuit. I was excited because the races were somewhat like races that professional track cyclists did on the velodromes. As Kevin carefully reviewed the rules for Miss-N-Out with us that day, I realized that these were tactical races designed to perfect our track skills. *Yay*, I thought. *Now, this should be good, clean fun.*

"OK, ladies, Miss-N-Out is an e-li-mi-na-tion race," said the IUSF official with a southern Indiana twang as he enunciated slowly to the eight of us, my heat of riders. We stood straddling our bikes on the start/finish line at the track. "Let's review the rules before we start, so everyone is clear on them. Each heat will begin with one pace lap around the track. After that pace lap, in *every* subsequent lap, the *last* rider to have her front tire cross the start/finish line will be *eliminated* from the competition. We will ask you—both over the loudspeaker and also by writing your number on a chalkboard in turn three—to leave the track without interfering with the remaining riders.

"Does everyone understand those rules? Be the last rider over the line and you're out! Only the top three advance to the next round. Any questions?"

We started off, and everyone nervously jockeyed for position. I knew that the best strategy involved saving energy by drafting behind others as much as possible. So I hopped in position behind two others. I was locked in within a half lap—I had the inner line on my left and riders in front of me and to my right. I waited for things to shift, but they remained constant with everyone holding their positions. I was boxed in. As we came to the first elimination lap, I felt a surge of panic. I cut wide on the final turn and zipped forward into the space in front of me. I stood and sprinted like crazy. Phew! I had made it out into the open in the nick of time.

Miss-N-Out was essentially a replay of this pattern over and over. I was in the first heat, and with only one team member from each team allowed per heat, that meant I had been the first to meet my fate from the Willkie Sprint team. After I was able to secure a top-three spot in my heat and advance to the next round, my teammates crowded around me with congratulations. I gave my teammates the only advice I could think of.

"Basically you never want to lead and get worn out pulling everyone else in your draft," I said. "All I can tell you is what worked for me. It's not a sophisticated strategy or rocket science or anything. Here's what you do: Hop in the middle of the pack behind others' draft. Getting boxed in is fine because you're protected. Start to freak out at turn three if you are boxed in. Look for a spot to jump into that will get you back into the open and then sprint like the dickens."

Following either common sense or my advice, my teammates all advanced to the semifinals. Amy was not racing, so it was Kristin, Louise, Kirsten, and me. In the semifinals, we ended up racing against each other as well as the better sprinters from all teams. Unfortunately, Kristin and Louise did not advance again, but Kirsten and I made it to the finals. We were a bit jittery going into the finals. I realized the toughest competition might come from my own teammate, whom I considered to be a better sprinter than I was.

"If you take me out, Kirsten, you better go on and win the whole thing," I said.

"Yeah, right, same thing if *you* knock *me* out," said Kirsten.

"Well, I'm more scared of you," I said, "than any other rider in there!"

Kristin laughed. "It's true," she said. "I would be afraid of Kirsten too. Your little legs go around so fast, girl! You are *both* so powerful."

"This is practice for the real sprint in the Little 500," said Kirsten, "so I don't think we should worry about eliminating each other a bit." She was right, of course. Honestly, I could not help but expect her to eliminate me and win the whole thing.

"That's right," added Kevin. "You girls need to just race as hard as you can. It's each woman for herself. No being soft on your teammates. This is great sprint training. Nothing else will be this much like the race. Pour your hearts into it. See what you guys can do!"

"I think I am just going to picture ol' Pirate chasing me down," I said, kidding but serious.

"Why didn't you tell me to do that earlier?" said Louise, perennially terrified of Pirate. "That would've gotten me into the finals!"

When we started the finals, it only took a half lap of posturing before we were flying along at a blistering pace. Both Kirsten and I survived the first sprint, but I knew that this final round would just keep amping up. Surviving each lap would take all my sprinting prowess. Since Kirsten was a crazy fast sprinter, I felt a little insecure about my own sprint. When we were on rides in the country, we would often do sprints to city-limit signs and other established points. Although it was usually close, generally Kirsten or Amy won the sign sprints.

I tried to take Kevin's words as inspiration and do nothing to assist Kirsten. I just rode my own race. I survived the second sprint. And then the third. With five cyclists left though, I got caught on the outside during the final turn and had to close a small gap, which left me fighting to not be the last wheel across the line. Unfortunately, I was. I slammed my fist onto my handlebars in disappointment and dropped from the pack.

I watched the next sprint from across the track as I was still on my bike. Kirsten had survived another elimination. *Yes! Will she win the whole thing?* I wondered. There were only three riders left. Fans and team members were cheering loudly, and we screamed for her as well. As fate had it, Kirsten was outsprinted by a small margin on the next lap.

Kirsten and I were particularly disappointed in our performance. Sometimes it feels worse to come close to winning than to go out early.

"Three of us in there and our highest finish was third," said Kirsten when she had regained her breath. "I am so sorry, you guys. I failed us." Kirsten always had lofty expectations of herself and was pretty hard on herself if she did not meet them.

"Are you kidding me? How can you girls be disappointed?" said Kevin. "Kirsten was third *out of about one hundred riders.* Come on, this day was a total success! We had two in the top five, and all four of you—our entire team—made the semifinals. You can't even tell me you are not happy with that."

"Kevin's right, Kirsten," said Kristin. "As a team overall, we did pretty darn well!" She smiled, and our energy became more positive. The day had, of course, been a good one for Willkie Sprint. With two weeks until race day, we had made a strong showing in which it was clear we were a team to beat.

"One more thing," said Kevin. "Speaking of the effort of the team overall, I just want you guys to give a little credit to Louise. She has pushed herself *be-yond.* And she is the only one of you that did not come in having already done years of competitive sports. She has put up with you guys and Amy," he continued, nodding toward Kirsten, Kristin, and me, "and let me tell you, in case you don't already know: you girls are intense. Anyway, great job today, Louise. You really rose to the occasion."

"Ahem, Kevin," said Kristin, "you might not know it, but *you* are pretty intense too. And Louise has also put up with you!" Kristin smiled at him. She was right: Kevin *was* intense. Between the two of them, Kristin and Kevin had poured hours—plus blood, sweat, and tears—into coaching us in this intramural race. Kristin even more hours in training. I loved that they were also making sure Louise got credit for how hard she had worked.

"Well, thanks, y'all," said Louise. I had never really heard anyone outside of films who had authentically used "y'all" and always found it endearing when Louise did. "Honestly, I am just trying to do my part. Keeping up with you all has been one of the hardest things I have ever done."

"You rock, Louise," said Kirsten, giving her a high five.

"Sorry to reveal your secrets, Louise," I said, "but I gotta share the details of your secret training."

Louise smiled but looked bewildered about what I might say. "Louise has become the speed champion of our dorm floor. She can get the Mini 500 trike moving like no other. You should see her!" Then I added, "No seriously, you guys probably don't even know, but Louise and I have taken a lot of bike rides just the two of us, and she's really worked hard. And we've had a lot of fun in this here Bloomington hill country," I said, adding a flourish of southern accent.

"Actually," said Louise, "I've pretty much loved getting into the sport of cycling. It's giving up the Pizza Express breadsticks and garlic butter that has been the hardest sacrifice for me!"

"They should call it 'Pizza Distress,'" said Kirsten, always ready to defend our junk food ban, "because that's for sure what your arteries are feeling when you guys order those. You should be thanking me, because your hearts are." And with that, we packed it up and left the track.

CHAPTER

"I HAVE A GREAT IDEA," said Rob, who was waiting when I got back to the dorm. "You were saying how you love stars, and well . . . so I thought we could go camping tonight. We can set up a tent in case it rains. It's not supposed to though. I was thinking, what better plan than—drumroll, bada bada boom—laying out and stargazing. In sleeping bags, under the night sky. What do you say?" He looked at me expectantly, but I am pretty sure he knew that he had me at stargazing.

"Wait, your race," he said. "I'm all excited about my little plan so I forgot to ask. You had your race. How did it go today for the Willkie Dominatrix? Are you too tired to camp?" I told him about the race and pondered his proposal for about two seconds flat. Miss-N-Out had involved hours of emotional energy, but the mental concentration and physical effort had not been too taxing. Plus, I always had energy for camping under the night sky.

"Well it *is* really warm today," I said. "I mean, it feels like summer. Otherwise, I'm not sure that I'd consider it. You know I hate being cold." Then, expecting the common response to me as a Wisconsinite, I added, "Don't say it. I know, I know . . . I'm from Wisconsin, which somehow, for everyone, means that I don't mind the cold. I don't really get that. Hello-o, maybe there's a reason that I am not living there right now. Anyway, don't you think it will get pretty cold overnight? Do you even know where to go?" We did see a lot of signs for state forests and campgrounds on our rides, but I had not paid attention to where they were.

"I checked it out," he said, "and it's supposed to be warm like this for a few days. Anyway, I will keep you toasty warm. Looking forward to it. Come on, I think we'll have a blast," he said. Rob had borrowed sleeping bags and a tent from his roommate, and Joe was willing to lend us his car. So, *Well, why not*, I thought.

I was born on August 21, during the annual κ-Cygnid and Perseid meteor showers that produce skies reminiscent of Van Gogh's *The Starry Night*. That start to my life seems to have left me with an overdeveloped appreciation for shooting stars, and celestial wonders in general, for that matter. In reading a recent assignment for Professor Sanders's class, I had been struck by Annie Dillard's line in *Pilgrim at Tinker Creek*:

> In the great meteor shower of August, the Perseid, I wail all day for the shooting stars I miss.

I knew exactly how she felt. Some August nights up at Sunday Lake, I had waited impatiently for the summer sun—so greedy in consuming the sky for nearly all of our waking hours—to set, thus allowing the sky to darken. Only then were the shooting stars finally visible. The irony was not lost on me: as a sun-lover, I have always been happy to bask in its glow and generally cheer as the days get longer in the springtime. Thus, even I myself was amused by my unusual desire for darkness to arrive, albeit just for that short week or so leading up to my birthday each year.

Sunday Lake was eight miles away from the nearest town, Minocqua, which only had a few thousand people anyway. On the lake, with no light pollution from the glow of a nearby city, we had pitch-black nights and perfect stargazing conditions. My sister and partner in crime, Molly, and I liked to camp out overnight on Eagle Island during the meteor showers and enjoy the show. We would load up the canoe with supplies and head out to pitch the tent after dinner. Then we would return to the mosquito-free cabin and wait for darkness to settle in. Not exactly wailing like Annie Dillard but definitely moaning a bit about how long it was taking for the sun to set.

"Oh, there's one," I'd say the moment we'd settled in our sleeping bags outside our tent. No sooner were those words spoken than Molly was shouting, "Look, over there! Did you see that one?" Followed by "WHOA! Super bright! Did you see that one?" And so on and so forth for hours until we couldn't keep our eyes open anymore. Since we knew those shooting stars came just once a year, we stayed up deep into the night. We might start by counting the shooting stars, but we would soon be bored of that.

It was not the number of shooting stars that interested us, just the fact that there were so darn many, all night long, for days. Each one felt special. Remembering how hard it seemed to finally close my eyes on the shooting stars, I laughed out loud reading Dillard's frustration that, at dawn, the blue dome of morning light clamped down over her "like a lid on a pot." I had shared the excerpt and my Sunday Lake stargazing sessions with Rob a few days earlier.

By the time Rob and I had loaded the car for camping, it was late afternoon. We headed to JL Waters, Bloomington's outdoors store. I loved it there. With beautiful wooden canoes hanging from the rafters, the place had a vibe somewhere between granola-crunching hippieville and Patagonia-gear hipness (all long before Patagonia was actually considered hip). We stood at the counter in the store studying a map and deciding between Yellowwood State Forest and Brown County State Park.

"Check out these town names," I said. "Gnaw Bone, Indiana. Story, Indiana. Stony Lonesome, Indiana. You have got to be kidding me. Can we please go to Brown County? We have got to check these places out! There's even a Nashville. Wow, this forest is huge." Starting about ten miles to the east of Bloomington, the dark green shading on the map indicated that trees essentially took over in a large expanse that amounted to one large forest, although it was labeled as two separate tracts named Yellowwood State Forest and Brown County State Park.

"Yeppers," said the clerk behind the counter, who had a little of that south central Indiana twang in his voice. "It's about 625 square miles of forested playground out that direction. You got every outdoor activity you can imagine available out there. Most students spend four years here in Bloomington and never even make it out there. Don't even know it's there."

"OK, well then," said Rob, determined not to be one of them, "I guess it's time to go check it out. Is there a place to camp that you'd recommend? Maybe somewhere we can hike into?"

"When, *today*?" The clerk looked surprised at our lack of planning. Then again, he was in his thirties or forties, so that explained it. "Aren't you guys heading out a bit late? The official campsites don't open for another month, but you could probably get away with camping anywhere you find some empty ground. It's pretty quiet this time of year. But today," he glanced at his watch, "well, you'll be lucky to set up camp before it gets dark unless you hit the road immediately." *People really do lose their spontaneity with age*, I thought. *Jeez.* I hoped not to be that way myself someday. We purchased the map and a few flashlights and headed off.

"That guy was probably thinking that we still had dinner to cook out there on a camp stove," I said as we pulled to a stop in front of Garcia's Pizza. Time to buy our dinner. I thought of what I had learned from my Italian TA, who had returned to Indiana after living in Florence for a year. She had told us about traditions related to food and eating in Italy and how the amazing pizza in Italy had ruined any enjoyment of eating it back here in the US. "I am pretty sure," I told Rob, "that no upstanding, self-respecting Italian would ever buy pizza from a joint that had a Spanish last name." We laughed but entered. Neither of us being Italian, we did not think twice about the unlikely marriage of Spaniards, or in this case, maybe Mexicans, and Italian food.

Garcia's Pizza might not have been the world's greatest, but Rob and I had become regulars since the day we learned that Hoagy Carmichael had written the famous song "Stardust" there in 1927. Carmichael, a famous piano jazz musician, was a Bloomington native. For many years, the building now housing Garcia's Pizza had been home to another establishment, the Book Nook. There, Carmichael had tapped out the notes to "Stardust" on an upright piano in the corner. The old piano no longer existed, but Garcia's had built a booth with comfortable bench seating there and posted a plaque commemorating the spot where Carmichael penned one of his most famous songs.

This plaque had been all that was needed for my inquisitive boyfriend to dive into research. Rob had informed me that the Book Nook had been a soda fountain, bookstore, and music venue all in one, but it was best described by Hoagy Carmichael himself in his biography, *Sometimes I Wonder*, as "a randy temple smelling of socks, wet slickers, vanilla flavoring, face powder, and unread books." Reading this description to me, Rob had impersonated whatever voice he had associated with Hoagy Carmichael, the young jazz musician enthralled by the Book Nook's charming, artistic, and seedy vibe.

"Sounds like our kind of place!" I said. I had to laugh, because it was true that our wandering around campus sometimes landed us in places that fit that description.

"Actually it was the Roaring Twenties," Rob said, "so probably it was such a hit because there was illegal boozing going on. This Book Nook place sounds like it was soda fountain on the outside, speakeasy on the inside." Carmichael's biography recounted how the Book Nook was a big draw for his contemporaries, in spite of, or maybe because of, its "dim [lighting], its scarred walls, its marked up booths and unsteady tables." The real draw may have been that the establishment thumbed its nose at the prohibition laws. It was known to be quite rowdy. The Book Nook's lore included their own commencement ceremonies, carried out in garish (rather than lavish) style and awarding fantastic degrees such as Master of Hearts, Doctor of Physique, Doctor of Discord, Eroticus, Vociferatissimus, Doctor of Yell, and Lord Mare of Hearts. Carmichael was a master of ceremonies, wearing, in lieu of cap and gown, a bathrobe and red-and-white-striped fez cap.

Herman B Wells, formerly IU's president and its chancellor that year, the very president who had greenlit the creation of the (men's) Little 500 race back in the 1950s, had himself been awarded the degree of Doctor of Nookology at one of the Book Nook commencement ceremonies. Despite having stepped into the ceremonial role of chancellor rather than serving as university president by the time I had arrived at IU, Wells was a cherished and beloved leader on campus. In his autobiography *Being Lucky*, he talked about the Book Nook's importance as a bustling hub of student activity, "a remarkable fertile cultural and political breeding place in the manner of the famous English coffee houses." The coffeehouse aspect was quite evident in the picture we unearthed of Hoagy Carmichael, seated at Book Nook's piano surrounded by a raucous-looking group.

"I wish we had a place like that to hang out," I said. As Rob had reported those facts to me on an earlier trip to the Hoagy Carmichael booth at Garcia's

Pizza, I thought that the true success of an establishment might be measured by how many people wrote glowingly about it in their autobiographies. At that point in the first year of my college career, I figured that the Indiana Memorial Union was the campus haunt most closely resembling our own version of the Book Nook. Either that or the Willkie dorm's bike room, our own "randy temple smelling of socks."

There was something though I had noted in those pictures of Hoagy Carmichael and friends crowded around the piano or celebrating the Book Nook commencement ceremonies in bathrobes. They were all men. Actually, they were all white men.

Women had long been admitted to IU, and the first, Sarah Parke Morrison, had graduated in 1869. African Americans had also long been admitted, with the first black man, Marcellus Neal, graduating in 1895 and the first black woman, Frances Marshall, in 1919. But for many years, both women and non-whites were few and far between. The IU School of Business, then called the School of Commerce and Finance, did not admit its first woman, Blanche McNeely, until 1922. In addition to Amelia, I add Sarah, Frances, and Blanche to my list for pushing the doors open to both opportunity and diversity for those of us who followed.

Garcia's was quite busy, and pizzas were coming out one after the other. We had planned on taking the pizza to-go. But waitstaff kept walking by with amazing-smelling pizza pies to deliver to tables. Between that scent and the hunger I had after my efforts in Miss-N-Out, we could not resist eating immediately. We decided to just sit in the Hoagy Carmichael nook and enjoy our pizza right away rather than box it up for the camping adventure.

"The pizza wouldn't have survived the car ride anyway," I said. "With that scent floating up at me, I would have definitely been doing some quality control sampling." I wiped my hands on my napkin and hit the bathroom—one last chance to take advantage of indoor plumbing. I was sure that we would not have any at our camping spot. Especially since we had no idea where we were heading. Our plan was just to head into the big forested "playground" that the clerk had referred to and find a spot from which to watch the stars.

As we drove out of town along State Road 46, the landscape became hillier and the surroundings more forested. The shadows grew longer as well. As the miles passed and no turnoffs became evident for state parks or camping, the concerned comment of the JL Waters's clerk rang in my head. I watched the sun setting, a fireball on the horizon, blazing from my side-view mirror. We had, in effect, left a bit late in the day, I supposed. Dusk was indeed falling rapidly all around us.

Finally, about fifteen miles out of town on the curving two-lane 46, we saw the first sign for Brown County State Park. It announced the Abe Martin Lodge. We thought it best to wait until we were more in the heart of the park and passed by the sign.

"Yeah, I remember that on the map," said Rob. "We can keep going a bit further." The warm meal, the quiet drive backlit by the sun setting, and the twilight had brought on a sudden bout of sleepiness. I fought off the urge to tell Rob that we had no time to search further with the sky's friendly fireball having gone below the horizon.

"All I remember is Stony Lonesome and Gnaw Bone," I said, "and I can only imagine what those two towns are like. Actually, I am not so sure I want to roll into either at nightfall. Let's save that for tomorrow and hit the Story Inn's brunch. For now, we just gotta beat the daylight." The clerk had told us that brunch at the Story Inn, a quaint restaurant and inn housed in the town's 1851 General Store, was not to be missed. But for now, we agreed to pull in at the next forest access road and find a spot to set up camp.

We drove a ways on the deserted road, searching for inspiration or, at that point, any decent pull-off parking spot. Honestly, the inability to see much outside the reach of our headlights made inspiration unlikely. At the first widening in the road allowing for us to park safely, we pulled over.

"Ranger Rick's Camping Gold Star Award goes to you for grabbing the flashlights and batteries," I said as we inserted the batteries and flicked them both on. Unable to see much, we grabbed our supplies and climbed over a little bluff. There we found a small field—slightly sloping ground but clear and open sky above.

"Looks like our spot," Rob said. "This will work perfectly. 'You'll be lucky to set up camp before dark!' Yeah, right." He conjured up our collective memory of the checkered-shirted clerk, and we laughed at his prophetic words. We clumsily set up our tent as darkness crept in. As I readjusted the stakes holding our tent fly down, Rob said he had forgotten something and dashed off toward the car. When he returned, he was hauling a big box.

"I got you something," he called out as he came near. "A present. I couldn't resist. It was too perfect for you." My heart beat with excitement, and I flushed. For some reason, getting gifts made me feel embarrassed. I never wanted to disappoint the gift-giver, so I felt pressure to genuinely like the gift, which is, of course, something I could not control. Either I liked it or I did not. If I opened a gift, I was always prepared to fake that I liked it and at the very least find something to appreciate about the gift. I was not skilled in telling a white lie. So I hoped I did not have to. That was the mental setup for being a bit nervous when I opened gifts.

"Wait, what did you haul way out here?" I said.

"OK," he said, placing the box on the ground in front of me. "Yeah, I had it hidden in the trunk. It kind of fits well with the setting. Open it. Carefully." As Rob shined his flashlight on the box, I heard in his voice a certainty that I would like the gift. I carefully opened the box to find a long black cylinder. With the eyepiece attached on the side of one end, I immediately recognized it as a Newtonian reflector telescope. It was beautiful—a Celestron with a wide cylinder, an equatorial mount making it easy to follow the path of the stars' circular arch through the sky, and a stable wooden tripod. Rob's generosity, the grandness of his gift, rendered me speechless. Other than an astonished "wow," I had no words for a few minutes. We assembled the telescope together in excited silence.

"Thank you. Thank you *so much*. It's *too much*," I said, hugging Rob as my words returned. "It's too generous. You shouldn't have." In equal parts, I thanked him and admonished him for spending too much. I imagined, based on its fine features, its weight, and its beauty, that the telescope cost a fair amount. And I felt uncomfortable with him having spent a bunch of money on a gift for me. Rob just smiled, making me feel that my comments rang on deaf ears.

"I'm glad you like it," he said, his eyes shining with the satisfaction of having pleased someone else, with the joy of giving. Well, yes, of course I liked it. In fact, I loved it. And I had been feeling the same way about him. *This guy is special*, I thought. He sat there smiling, happy to have found the perfect gift for me. And it was. No faking required. We set up the telescope and took advantage of the nautical twilight, the magic moment when the color fades from the sky and the celestial bodies and stars become visible in increasing profusion.

"Hey, let's see if we can focus on Venus and Jupiter," I said, staring through the eyepiece and trying to bring them into focus, "to see if they are still in conjunction." I had learned about the open observatory nights at the Kirkwood Observatory on campus while taking my astronomy class the previous semester. A month earlier, we had gone and observed an event that only happens every twenty-four years. The two brightest planets in the sky were in conjunction, with Venus passing just 2.2 degrees from Jupiter. That March night at Kirkwood Observatory, we had witnessed the colorful stripes of Jupiter's swirling gasses and the bright white of Venus's sulfuric acid clouds.

I took aim at the pair of planets, which appeared as a pair of bright and steady stars in the western sky. With the telescope, we were able to pick them out in nice detail. We followed them over the next few hours, until they went below the horizon one by one, alternating that with checking out the few constellations we knew by heart. We played around with the telescope until we were too cold to resist the pull of our sleeping bags anymore. We chatted as we lay there watching the night sky rich with celestial beings on display.

"Hey, thank you," I said. "For the telescope. But more than that. For showing up in my world." Rob pulled me closer, and we kissed. Eventually we fell asleep snuggled closely under the sky.

Convinced we had left civilization behind, it came as a huge shock to be abruptly awoken several hours later by a beam of light and the sound of a motor approaching.

"Holy crap, it's coming straight for us," Rob said as he stared toward the light, which appeared to be the headlights of a car. I opened my eyes and groggily recalled where we were.

"Oh my God, we have to move! Fast," I said, jumping up and pushing down the sleeping bag. I stared down but was unable to tell in the dark: "So, wait, did we set up our tent right on a dirt road or something?" We had fallen asleep outside of our tent, which was set up behind us.

We stood frozen for a second, literally like deer caught in the headlights, staring at the approaching vehicle. Then, in a frantic, frenzied moment, we both leapt off to the side and tried to get our bearings. Just then, as quickly as it had appeared and scared the bejesus out of us, the approaching car veered slightly to the right and swung past us, about thirty feet away. It curved out of sight past the bluff, and a few seconds later, we saw its taillights slowly disappear into the distance. For the second time that evening, I was so stunned that my words failed.

"Damn! So we must have parked right before the road curves," said Rob, piecing it all together, "and then we walked to this meadow, basically staying right along the road without realizing it." Having survived the scare intact, the gravity of the situation lifted and we broke out in giggles.

"So much for our big camping getaway from the modern world. I thought we were dead ducks," I said, my ability to speak returning. "In the end, we are basically camping right next to the road. We're such idiots!" We laughed at our own stupidity in arriving late and not taking the time to investigate our surroundings better before choosing our spot and pitching our tent. As we lay there dozing off again, I opened my eyes and sat back up. I wanted to check on the telescope.

"Let's name it, the telescope. How about 'Leo'?" I said, naming the telescope for my astrological sign. I moved Leo farther from the road and jumped back into the warmth of the sleeping bag. Then it occurred to me that I should give credit to the clerk at JL Waters for trying to save us from exactly the type of situation that had just happened.

"I think we might have just discovered what they mean when they say that youth is wasted on the young," I said, eyes closed but smiling to myself in the dark as we snuggled back into our sleeping bags just off that country road in Brown County State Park. "Re-goodnight." Luckily, it was a relatively deserted road within the park, so we slept through until morning without further disruption.

The next weekend, we had Team Pursuit, the final race of the Little 500 Series. It was an important opportunity to see how we stacked up as a team, just six days before the big day, the women's Little 500. Team Pursuit was raced as team versus team. We had to draw on our experience with riding in a paceline.

"OK. This is it," said Kevin as we prepared to head over to the track. "You have one shot to make the finals. Ten laps, all out. We are racing against whatever opponent they assign us but also against the clock. The two fastest teams—*only the two fastest teams*—make it to the finals."

"No matter who you are paired with," added Kristin, "you have to race your little legs off to get one of the top two times if you want to make the finals. They record everyone's times, and the fastest two advance to the championship match where they race for the win." She looked at us intently.

"I know we can make it if everyone is *on*," said Kristin, "but remember the time trial out at Morgan-Monroe State Forest? Remember what we learned out there? Teamwork is everything. It'll be the same thing on race day. Take care of each other. The team time is based on when the *third rider's wheel* crosses the finish line. Use all four riders as long as you can. Louise, pull hard early."

"You've got this, girls. Been training for it all year," said Kevin. "Now let's get over to the track. Do a few hard efforts on your ride over there to warm up." We headed out, wearing our team jackets with our matching Willkie Sprint T-shirts underneath. We chatted, joked, and sprinted against one another up all the rises on our way to the track.

Pedaling up the entrance drive from Fee Lane to the Bill Armstrong Stadium, we made our final effort, passing by other riders and teams who had not chosen to sprint up the long hill. They had more oxygen available for speaking, made clear by their cheers, cajoling, and catcalls to us as we zoomed past.

"Save a little for the race!"

"Guess who is gunning to win today?"

"Kirsten's beating you, Kerry!"

"Nice legs, you get those riding?"

"Hup! Hup! Hup!"

"Looking good, good-lookin'!"

Compliments and insults were hurled our way as we barreled up the climb to the track. The members of the other teams had been our companions for months at the track. During that time, we had learned track skills, perfected our exchanges, and shared laughs. We were united in participating in a first for female students, in training hard day after day, and in dreaming of pulling off the win. Together, we had gone from being total rookies to new cyclists to competitors. The camaraderie that we had enjoyed at Bill Armstrong Stadium every day over the previous six weeks was an unexpected bonus of competing in the Little 500. Riding in endless circles on cinder together, the hundred-plus female riders comforted each other after our falls, bantered endlessly, and puffed our chests out. We had become friends. Some were better or closer friends than others, yes. But if I saw anyone I recognized from the track on campus, I always took the time to greet her, maybe asking how things were going or whether she would be at the track later.

Only one team would win the Team Pursuit that day. Only one team would win the inaugural Little 500 race six days later. Regardless of whoever actually won, the real point was that we had all won in a sense, just by participating. We were all part of making the first year of the women's race successful. Together, our dedication to training and love of the Little 500 experience had proven that women deserved to be given the same opportunities as men. The riders of the inaugural race had grabbed hold of the equal opportunity and gotten maximum benefit from what the Little 500 offered. The Thetas and the host of women fighting prior to and alongside them, well, it turns out they were right. The friendships within and between teams were both an added bonus and the most poignant part of the experience.

"Did you hear all the grief I took?" said Kirsten after we caught our breath. "Sue yelled out, 'Your shoelaces are caught in your chainring!' No respect, I tell you."

I told her that the comments got worse after she passed and that no one was spared.

"Serves us right, I guess, for racing by everyone," I said, because it did. "We probably looked so cocky."

"Well, it worked," said Louise. "I am totally warmed up now. Can't do any more of that sprinting stuff till we are in the race, or I won't have any energy left!"

"Yup, that's it," said Amy. "In fact, we can just skip the race. I got my warm-up and workout in, all at once. Game over, folks. We can just ride back to the dorm if you guys are ready."

"It is definitely no fun riding these track bikes on any sort of incline," I said, feeling happy to have arrived at the flat ground of the track. Chatting away, we jumped on the track and rode some more warm-up laps.

Luckily we had drawn an early heat. The Team Pursuit race pits one team against another in a ten-lap race. Teams are randomly paired. Each team lays their bikes on the track, exactly opposite one another in the first and third corners. The teams must then stand twenty feet away from where their bikes lay. When the IUSF official fires the starting gun, bam!, both teams run to their bicycles, mount them, and take off on their ten-lap race.

"Kevin and I will each be standing on the infield," said Kristin as we waited our turn, watching the first heat. Two sorority teams were racing, one slowly advancing toward the other. We heard the riders of one team shouting at each other as they passed. "Leave the yelling to us when you are out there. We'll be in opposite corners shouting at you. Kev'll be giving you splits."

"Hopefully you'll be giving us encouragement, not just shouting," said Louise.

"No, no, shout at us! Tell me to get my fat ass moving," said Kirsten, and we all shared a laugh. As she was not much more than skin and bones, that was the last comment that anyone would lob her way.

"I'll leave that to Kevin," said Kristin. "I'm just giving love and encouragement."

"Listen," said Kevin, "this race is the one that shows which teams have the depth to be competitive on race day. I am hoping to see you guys catch the sorority by the tenth lap. Just make that your goal." The earlier heat finished, and the riders in our heat were instructed to take the track.

"Finally," said Amy, as we lined the bikes up in the order that we had agreed on for starting our paceline. "I am ready to get this over with."

"Me too," I said. "Let me know right away if anyone comes off our paceline. Should we just agree to shout out 'off' if it happens?" We agreed and headed to the infield to hear our race instructions.

"This is a race against the clock," said the IUSF official. "You will have another team racing at the same time, and most will work to catch them. But, remember, the only thing that advances you to the championship race is your time. Got that? Race against the clock, then. You're gonna start at the chalked line on the infield. No one moves till I fire the starting gun in the middle. Questions? If not, let's go."

"Race against the clock, then, is it?" I said, mimicking the official as we walked to our start line. I looked at the others and saw that everyone had their game faces on. Time to get serious. "Let's do this," I said. With that, we stood, a bit crouched like sprinters, ready to go. We watched the official raise his start gun, and bam! We were off!

I sprinted so hard to my bike that I nearly skidded on the cinders and fell when I reached it. *Now, go!* I told myself as we all hopped on our bikes and jammed on the pedals to get up to speed. I fell into line second as was our plan. No one immediately shouted "Off," meaning we had managed to get up to speed together. From there, the goal was simple: to keep it rolling as fast as possible, rotating through at the front of the paceline as smoothly as possible. For once, we managed to do just that.

As we snaked around the track, we started to catch glimpses of the other team in the far corners as we entered the straightaways. The carrot always draws the horse, and we sped up, trying to reel them in. I went into hyperfocus, that zone where time seems to slow down, the current effort is all that exists, and you are only minimally aware of your surroundings. Suddenly, the other team was right in front of us. So was the end of our tenth lap. We had caught the other team, right on the buzzer.

"Couldn't have done any more," said Amy, still catching her breath as she cruised up to me on our warm-down lap. We rolled to a stop next to Kevin and Kristin and regrouped with the others.

"Fastest time so far today," said Kevin. "Nice job. Now we can sit and watch people try to beat it."

"With our fingers crossed," Louise said. "I am still shaking from that effort." I was too.

"Now I know what they mean when they say you're in the zone," I said. "I was super focused, like nothing else existed."

"Well, that's how you need to be on race day," said Kirsten. "Your last pull was breaking my legs to stay on. Helps that you're so dang tall and have that huge draft—that's the zone I was loving." I had heard that comment before. Everyone loved riding behind me because I blocked all the wind so thoroughly with my height.

Kristin had brought some blankets, and we sat in the bleachers they had been building over the past month to accommodate the Little 500 crowds. I guess the stands were added every year, and they doubled the stadium's capacity by replicating the size of the permanent structure on the opposite side. As we watched their construction during track practice, I did wonder if they would actually fill all that seating. It seemed that darn near every student would need to come to fill all those seats. That day during Team Pursuit, they were relatively empty. The only pre–Little 500 race to draw much of a crowd had been Qualifications. Sitting up in the new bleachers, we hung out watching to see if we made the finals from behind our pit on the backstretch.

Once in a while, we'd yell some encouragement to friends from other teams as they zoomed by.

"OK, you guys better go take a little spin and get your legs warmed up again," said Kevin when it looked like no one would knock us out of contention for the championship race. We went as far as the large parking lot at the IU Memorial (football) Stadium down below, where we rode around in circles for a while.

"It's you guys versus Notorious," said Kristin, who had descended on her bike to find us. "The finals are in twenty minutes. Come on, we better get back up to the track." We had gone faster for ten laps than anyone else, but Notorious had essentially equaled our time. Now we would race them, team versus team in the finals. Objectively we had done well in all the Little 500 Series races but had not won any of them. This was our last chance. Only today's race, the finals of Team Pursuit, remained before Little 500 race day. The Thetas had placed fifth, so they were out, much to our relief.

This time, I was nervous. We all were. It was the championship match. Notorious had some strong cyclists. As we lined up, crouched and waiting for the starting gun, I noticed my right leg shaking a little bit. Was I nervous or cold? Both. *Ten laps*, I told myself, *only ten. Get in the zone.*

Bam! The starting gun launched us into action. Once we were up and riding, we pulled unevenly, each of us trying to push powerfully at the front but gauging our teammates' abilities to stay on the pace differently.

"Off!" Kirsten shouted four laps in, and then again, "Louise is off!" Our plan was to let whoever was lagging fall off the back eventually since the team's time was calculated based on the third rider. But was four laps in too early? I was at the front and slowed a touch. Louise fought back on to the wheel. When I dropped off the front, rotating to the back of the paceline, I jumped into the gap that had opened between her and Kirsten, making it easier for her to stay on. Amy's pace was fierce, and both Louise and I fought to stay on the tail end of our paceline.

I was hoping to enter the zone that I had found in our earlier heat but felt like this attempt was awkward. I was unable to manage the same degree of focus and concentration. I rode too hard at the front, dropping my teammates, and then due to making such an effort, struggled to reenter the rear of the paceline. We dropped Louise. I felt that it was my fault. I ruminated but tried to stay present and in the race. And so it went. *Just keep pedaling hard*, I told myself, trying to get in a rhythm that never arrived.

Kirsten, Amy, and I crossed the finish line, each making a final sprint that almost brought us parallel with one another.

"Aiiiye!" Kirsten yelled as we passed the line. I looked up from my sprint, searching for Notorious to see if they had finished yet. I thought I saw them finishing just then. A few seconds after we had. *So we had . . . won?* I glanced ahead and down the track as we completed the turn and saw Kevin, standing still at the end of the straightaway with both arms raised over his head. We had pulled it off. A win!

As we caught our breath, we let out some squeals of excitement.

"I felt horrible," I said. "I felt like I never got in a rhythm. I couldn't concentrate. I was all jerky." I was letting loose a rapid-fire list of apologies.

"What are you talking about?" Kirsten stopped me. "We won! It might not have been pretty, but we did it." She laughed, and I did too. We were riding a few warm-down laps. Louise caught up with us, apologizing like I had. Kirsten stopped her as well.

"Jeez," she said. "We did it! We did fine. You guys are so hard on yourselves." Those were ironic words coming from the teammate who was perhaps hardest of all on herself. Kirsten wore her heart on her sleeve. If she was relaxed, finally happy with our effort and first-place finish, then we all should be.

"More than fine, Kirsten," said Amy. "We won! And all I could think during the whole race was, I never had to pee so bad. I think it's all that water I drank. Kirsten, you got me so worried about staying hydrated." Smiles won over our facial expressions. As the Notorious team members approached, we congratulated them and told them that having to pee was our secret weapon.

CHAPTER

"FOUR DAYS AND COUNTING till race day," said Kevin the following Monday toward the end of track practice. "We have to turn the bikes in for inspection on Wednesday, so Thursday is a rest day for everyone. Track is closed."

"Except for me; I get to come out and put up our pit boards," said Kristin. "Kev and I were thinking . . . Let's do a team dinner at a nice restaurant Thursday night. Kind of a psych-up team meal. We can see how you guys clean up."

Louise clapped and gave a "hurrah!" at the idea of dressing in something other than spandex for an evening.

Kevin had been thinking about ways he could communicate with us during the race as we flew by the pit. The Theta coach and some other coaches had started bringing small handheld whiteboards to the track. During Team Pursuit, these coaches would write something like "+3 sec" to indicate the team was three seconds slower than the other team. Kevin thought the whole idea was farcical.

"I don't get how these coaches expect a rider who is all focused on the race and riding along inches away from others in a pack to look over and take the time to read a little note they are holding up," he said. "I think it's hilarious, actually. Can't believe they're doin' it. Seriously." He smiled and shook his head back and forth. He devised his own way of sending us messages without requiring us to look over and read a written message as we raced by.

"OK, there are two things I want to tell you: first, how many laps till you come in for an exchange, and second is whether it's a one- or two-bike exchange. That's it. One arm straight up means in one lap you need to come in for an exchange. Two arms straight up means you come out in two laps," he said, demonstrating. "Then comes the second piece of information: One arm out to the side means you come in for a one-bike exchange. Two arms straight out means it's a two-bike exchange." We practiced a bit, getting used to his signals.

"You imagining the win?" said a coach in a neighboring pit, as Kevin stood with two arms straight up, sending a signal to Kirsten to come in for an exchange in two laps, but looking to anyone who did not know our signals like he had just won something. "Don't be so sure about a victory," said the other coach with a smirk.

"I know, I know," said Kevin, kidding him back, "it's *your* race. But let me just *pretend for a second, one second.* Just one imagined moment of glory." The group of us standing there, we Willkie Sprint members and the riders from the other team, smiled at each other. *Men.*

After dinner that night, I got busy on the mission of finding my dad and sister a hotel room. Dad wanted to come see this race he had heard so much about during my phone calls home. He also remembered *Breaking Away* quite fondly and had driven me batty by continually asking questions like whether the Cutters, the team from the movie, were based on a real team; whether they were actually townies; and whether the Cutters still raced. The answer was complicated: No, they weren't based on a team called the Cutters (they were actually based on the screenwriter's own fraternity team). Yes, there would be a Cutters team racing in the men's race that year, but it was not the Cutters "townie" team Dad expected from the movie's storyline. All the teams who raced in the Little 500 were comprised of undergraduate students, whereas the film's Cutters were townies, not students. Proud of their townie status, they had chosen the name Cutters to honor the local blue-collar workers who cut limestone. The success of the film had inspired the creation of a team named after the movie's own Cutters. Only these real-life Cutters—the ones Dad would see when we watched the men's race—were all IU students.

I had not realized that the Little 500 drew such an influx of visitors that hotel bookings needed to be made months in advance. So there I was, with the phone book open to the yellow pages listing all the hotels, calling them one after the other on the telephone in our dorm room. Not having any luck finding a room for Dad and Ann, I was getting flustered when Rob stopped by.

"Hello. You coming to study?" said Rob as he sat down on the trike.

"No, I am freaking out," I said. "I was supposed to get my dad a hotel room, and there is *nothing*. I can't believe it." I was literally starting to sweat from the effort. "I can't take any more rejection," I said. I had been kidding, but I actually did feel the urge to cry while speaking those words. My eyes welled up, but I held back the tears. I figured Rob probably regretted stopping by for a visit.

"Hey, why don't you take a romp on the trike?" I said in the cheeriest tone I could manage. "We only have it for a few more days." I hoped that would allow me to regain my cool. Instead, he scooped up the telephone receiver and took over the job of speaking with hotel receptionists. I dialed the hotels, one by one, and he asked for the room reservation. Occasionally, he used an accent or goofy voice.

"Thank you," I said, truly thankful that he had turned my task from miserable to fun. Then, as an afterthought, "Stop with the voice though. What if they don't offer a room because they think you are a weirdo?"

A few calls later, we were down to calling out-of-town establishments. We finally found something, but it was way out past Lake Monroe in Bedford. I snapped it up since it was the first hotel vacancy I had found, period. But I dreaded telling my dad that after driving seven hours to get to Bloomington, they were staying out of town and would have to drive half an hour back and forth.

"Do you really think we should come?" Dad had asked me a few days earlier. My mom would stay home with my sister Molly, who had a high school soccer game. Dad was thinking of coming down with my other sister, Ann. "I mean if you guys won the Team Pursuit race, you might have a shot at winning the whole thing." I had shushed him on any chance of winning but definitely encouraged him to come. And now I had failed him on the hotel room. Who knew? According to all the hotel receptionists, *I* should have known. "Rooms? No, no, we're all booked. You know, it's the Little 500 race this weekend" was what I, then Rob, heard in succession.

"I don't really get it," I said to Rob, as we walked to the Union. "This is a city of over fifty-five thousand people plus like thirty thousand college students. IU has big basketball games and stuff all the time, and the Little 500 race of all things takes the hotels over capacity?" We had heard that it was a huge party weekend. MTV had come for the past few years and built the reputation of the Little 500 as the "World's Greatest College Weekend."

"I just read in the *IDS* this morning," said Rob, referring to the *Indiana Daily Student* newspaper, "that there were over thirty-two thousand people at the race last year. And MTV is coming again this year. The IU officials, well, they warned students to be safe since there were some hooligan acts last year."

My own sampling of friends showed why hotels were at capacity. Rob had invited a friend from his hometown, Karen had both her parents and her boyfriend coming from Cincinnati to watch her in the Mini 500, all my teammates had their families coming, and nearly everyone on our dorm floor had incoming guests. All planned on fully partaking in the shenanigans. The week was building toward a slam-bam finish.

The next day, Kevin summoned us to a bike team meeting after the track hours, under the pretext of washing bikes. As might have been predicted, a raucous water fight ensued. Then we toweled down and splayed out in the bike room, where the heat—at other times oppressive—felt great and cured our shivering. Kevin turned serious.

"I gotta say it's been an experience coaching you girls," he said. "You're just a super-talented and super-dedicated group, and that made my job easy. In retrospect, I didn't give our guys' team enough energy because it was just so exciting having this set of individuals. I feel a little bad about that for the guys, but the point is, I knew you girls had a true shot at being tops. And that was confirmed, over and over, as you did so well in all the Little 500 Series races."

"Kevin, don't jinx us!" said Amy. "There're a lot of strong teams. I don't know how anyone is going to beat the Thetas!" The rest of us nodded and added other insecurities onto Amy's comment. We listed individual riders and teams that we feared and revered.

"Remember, you guys just won Team Pursuit," said Kristin, in response to our insecurities. "I think that's like the single biggest indicator of who will do well on race day."

"Listen," Kevin said, "let's not get all agitated. Believe. That's all." He shifted, in his seat and in the conversation.

"I called this meeting because there is something I want to tell you all," Kevin said, "because it feels weird to me that you don't know. I mean, Kristin knows, but only her." He took a breath, and there was a pregnant pause in the conversation. All eyes were on Kevin. I felt the gravity of his words before he spoke them, just from his expression.

"Remember when we had the Prologue, the street race up fraternity row? Remember how I couldn't make it, so Wes was there with you?" he said. "Well, that's because I was at my mom's funeral that day." You could have heard a pin drop. My body had a visceral reaction, a shiver that worked up my spine and forward through my chest, almost as if it coursed through my torso—through my heart.

Noo, I wanted to say out loud, but his news had rendered me speechless, and the word screamed in my head and seemed to ricochet down throughout my body. Words that change everything are almost always horrible ones.

"Kevin, I am sorry," said Amy. "Oh my God."

"Kevin . . ." Louise started but couldn't finish.

"Jeezus," said Kirsten, "why didn't you say something? You didn't have to coach us through this. We would have figured it out. Kristin would have done it. And you could have focused on your family."

None of our minds could get around it. *Kevin's too young to lose his mom*, I thought. Of course, we all were. *His mom must have been too young too*. I had these thoughts but could not voice a word. I was struggling to process the news. We all were.

"I didn't tell you guys this to weigh you down with it," Kevin said. "I don't want to do that. Not at all. It's something I'm dealing with. It's not easy. I knew my mom was struggling, but you never expect this. Our family was . . . my parents . . . we were like *Leave It to Beaver*. My mom . . . God bless her."

I was sitting next to Kevin on the floor. I put my arm around him and squeezed hard. I wondered what had happened, but the bottom line was that his mom was gone. No one pried. Everyone shed tears. All we could offer was support, words, and hugs. None of that could bring his mom back. Nothing could. And that was the cold, hard fact that he had dealt with for the past month and would deal with for years to come.

"I'm gonna wear a pink shirt," he said, "on race day. To honor her ... I want to wear pink for her. And I wanted you guys to know. That's all. I'm OK. I just wanted to let you know about it. I don't want it to weigh you down. But right now, it's where I am coming from. And Kirsten, I am totally up for coaching. It's giving me something positive to focus on. I need that right now."

When our emotional meeting ended, we had somehow been solidified as a group. We were a team, but more than that, we were friends. That was what really mattered. All that mattered. As emotionally destroyed as I was by Kevin's news, I was also glad that he had wanted to share it with us. Deflated, I headed back to my room. I hoped Karen was not there, and I hoped that Rob did not stop by. Everything about my normal life seemed superfluous. I wanted to crawl in a ball and mourn the woman I had never met.

Karen and I were enrolled in a second class together that semester, in addition to Modern Dance. Given my experience in the women's literature course, I thought that we might like Women in American Society W200, offered by the Women's Studies Department, and got Karen to sign up with me. In the end though, it was pretty depressing. Basically we learned about the history of women being downtrodden and the modern-day vestiges of this treatment. Women made significantly less in the exact same jobs as men, I learned, all over the economy. We learned that women did a highly disproportionate share of unpaid work, for which they received little recognition. We learned that cultural representations and sexualization of women reinforced bias and even oppression because of the dominance of male-centered viewpoints. In other words, we learned all sorts of unsavory truths about being female.

We left class feeling dejected. Could it be true that we were destined to be treated as inferior? Honestly, little of what we learned jibed with my experience so far in life. Being presented with factual truths about how all of humanity treats your sex as inferior was an education that I did not really enjoy getting, and a real downer to boot.

Surprisingly, I never really related what I had learned in that class to the experience that I was having on my bike. Arriving one year earlier on campus, I might have felt the sting of gender inequality firsthand. I might have fought as they had—the Thetas, Jill from Alpha Phi Epsilon, and Debbie Satterfield, who was now coaching the Stonies' team because the race had come a year too late for her. Various circumstances, including my family, my progressive hometown, and even the timing of my arrival at IU had conspired to keep me from experiencing the gendered injustices that others, even many from my own generation, had. Sitting in that Women's Studies class, I took in the lessons with skepticism. Instead, I should have thanked my lucky stars.

Walking back to the dorm after class with Karen, we discussed that day's lecture, which dealt with sexuality and the gender politics affecting abortion laws. Another version of men deciding for women, in this case taking away women's opportunity to have a choice. The class was intense and not my favorite, but it did get us thinking.

"I have been thinking a lot about Kevin's mom," I said. "He told us she was like June Cleaver, Beaver's mom in *Leave It to Beaver*. Guess that we all were raised watching that show. That family was like the perfect family. June was the homemaker extraordinaire, you know, and Ward was the working dad. It's weird because they feed us that example of a model family. But sometimes maybe it's not."

"It never works quite that way, girl," said Karen, "which is why *it's a TV show*, and you've never really met anyone like June and Ward in real life."

"It's the whole thing about propagating cultural stereotypes, I guess," I said. I didn't know anything about Kevin's family, really. His comment the other day had just been his way of saying that he had a great childhood. I had one too, so I knew what he was talking about. June and Ward Cleaver and the other examples from TV really had a strong hold on us, particularly as kids. It gave me a context in which to understand my professor's comments about the power of cultural stereotypes and how they box us in. On that note, MTV was coming for Little 500? I hoped that they covered the women's race too, projecting the image of college women racing their hearts out, thirty teams of them.

CHAPTER

"PERFORMING AT OUR BEST tomorrow means eating carbohydrates to-night," said Kirsten, holding court just outside the entrance to Willkie North as we gathered the evening before the race. We were heading to our team dinner. "Not the time for a big steak. Sorry, Amy. We have to avoid fat and protein because tomorrow we need the glycogen stores in our muscles to be totally full."

"OK, Kirsten, got it," said Kristin. "Let's just go though. You can give us an earful from your high-level nutrition course as we are on our way. You guys have a big day coming up. We are heading out for Italian, folks. And Willkie is covering this with the last of our budget."

"Yay. Who says that there is no free lunch?" I said. "Tonight, we're getting free dinner. Nice job on choosing Italian. Kirsten can order us all big pasta meals so we max out our carbo-loading opportunity." I was excited to hear that we were headed to Leslie's Italian Villa, the same place Rob and I had gone a few months back on our first date. I hoped it was a good omen for our race just as it had been for my relationship with him. I wanted to get Kirsten's nutritional blessing to order the lasagna again.

We ordered carbo-loading meals but no drinks—even Kevin and Kristin, who were of drinking age, stayed on the dry side in solidarity with our self-imposed drinking ban. Kevin reviewed our strategy, which was based on all the splits he had been taking the past month. He had figured out how long each of us could sustain a specific pace and wanted to keep us each on the bike as long as possible to minimize the number of exchanges. Our competitive juices were running high. No alcohol was necessary—we were giddy with excitement. The other part of our strategy was to stay close to the Thetas, so Kevin advised us to watch them in the bunch.

Hope was so thick in the air around our table, you could have bottled and sold it. We had worked hard for months and centered our lives around training for this race. The following afternoon, the long-awaited inaugural women's Little 500 race would finally happen. All our hard work would be put to the test. Underlying our giddiness and hope was our sense that we had a shot at doing well. After we had finished eating our meals, Kevin flipped his intensity switch on. Actually, no, this was something different; I might better label this his motivation switch.

"I started to see, as you all started getting results in the first Little 500 Series races," he said, "exactly what team had fallen into my lap when I agreed to coach for our dorm. I already knew, from day one, that I had lucked out to have such amazing athletes. You guys really are like a coach's dream team. Actually, you don't even need much coaching since you are all so motivated. But then we started collecting all these top finishes at the various races, and I knew that we had something special.

"I have been telling Kristin for the past month," he said, "that we can win this race."

"That's true," Kristin said, nodding. "Kevin's been logging other teams' splits too, and you guys stack up on top. You know, I think because you are all freshmen maybe, you are the dark horse in the race. Everyone knows that you're talented riders and that you have the potential to do really well. But honestly, I don't think anyone expects you to win. You are the perfect underdogs."

"There's really just one thing that I want to say tonight, one thing you should take away from this dinner," said Kevin, pausing. Silence settled over us as we waited to hear that one thing. *"Don't be afraid to win."*

"Everyone has always acted like this race is owned by the Theta team," he said. "I like the Thetas a lot. And they did a lot to bring this race to life. Honestly, they deserve all the credit in the world for doing that. But the best team will win the race tomorrow. The best team *should* win the race tomorrow. And I think that'll be you girls. So don't hold yourselves back. The Thetas don't deserve to win any more than we or anyone else does.

"Don't. Be. Afraid. To. Win," he said again, slowly enunciating the catchphrase he had created to open our minds to the possibility of winning the race. "I want every single one of you to think about that. Just embrace the idea of winning. You've earned your fitness and your track skills, and you deserve it."

We exchanged excited looks with one another. Kevin's words resonated with us. Personally, I did feel indebted to and in awe of the Thetas. From the first time I had met the Theta riders, I half-imagined, half-expected them to win the Little 500. Somehow Kevin's words freed me to imagine a different result. My teammates and I smiled broadly at each other, no one saying much. Something had shifted.

We went on to discuss our race strategy. Kevin strongly believed that we were capable of lapping the entire pack of riders, that is, breaking away from the others and steadily gaining an advantage that grew until we reentered at the rear of the group. Any team capable of doing so would have a great shot at winning because they would always remain one lap ahead of everyone else. But a team had to be incredibly strong to pull off lapping everyone. Plus, this strategy assumed that the riders would stay together in a pack, and no one knew if the women would do so because of the variety of skill and talent levels among the teams. Kevin was convinced that based on our splits in recent weeks, a hard effort early on could pay off by putting us a lap ahead of everyone else. He and Kristin thought it was worth trying.

The idea was this: We would wait until the flurry of the initial laps, which would be fast and maybe jittery, calmed into a rhythm. Then, we would look for the opportunity to attack the pack of riders and get a gap that we could steadily grow into a full lap advantage on the others. Reentering the pack from behind would allow us the advantage of "resting" in the slipstream of the others after having made the big effort to lap the pack.

Amy and Kirsten were downright giddy at the idea. Louise looked worried about the plan. Lapping the pack was something I had never considered. Like Louise, I felt more guarded about burning the energy that it might take for us to attempt lapping the pack. I worried about not having enough energy to do well if our strategy did not pan out. What if we depleted all our energy trying to lap the group and then did not have enough left in our legs to do well in a sprint finish if we failed? Kevin assured us that he would coach us through whatever result arose. We were going to try to lap the pack. We committed to racing boldly, no matter what.

I was restless that night as I tried to fall asleep in my loft. Karen was out kicking off the weekend of partying. Rob was busy entertaining his good high school friend Jim, who had shown up from out of town for the World's Greatest College Weekend. I had just one class to attend the next morning, and then my dad and sister would arrive after lunch sometime. I was nervous and excited. *Don't be afraid to win.* I had hoped all year to do well in the race. There had been a bit of press, mostly in the local newspapers and in the *Indiana Daily Student*, about the women's inaugural race, and essentially all of it focused on the Theta team. They were the heirs apparent to the women's edition of the Little 500. Willkie Sprint was barely mentioned and never prominently.

Earlier, Kristin had told us that being the underdog was an advantage. All eyes would be on the Thetas. Could this mean an opportunity for us in some way? For the first time, I closed my eyes and imagined what it would feel like to win the Little 500 race. Not the glory at the end of the race. Not the trophy and the celebration. I pictured it actually happening, during the race. In my mind's eye, I just slipped away from the pack, somehow, some way. Maybe by faking that I was going out for an exchange. Maybe by following the Theta rider who sprinted out for an exchange and then sprinting off her wheel as she slowed to pass off the bike. Maybe by riding right off the front of the pack when things were strung out. Maybe by taking advantage and slipping away in a moment of chaos. I pictured all of these scenarios. Lapping the pack? I pictured us doing that too. Doing so calmed my restlessness. It also sealed my determination.

Growing up, I had been fed a steady diet of positive thinking. My parents had met at Marquette University and raised us Catholic as they themselves had been. But my mom had always been more interested in spirituality than in religion. She went to a holistic doctor, did tarot card readings, and took trips to learn from shamans in both Peru and Chile. One of her greatest interests was in the mind-body-spirit connection. She read, and read to us, about the power of the mind. Mom's strongest advice to her five children was that we could do whatever we wanted if only we believed.

When I was about twelve years old, she made a little sign and taped it on the bathroom mirror. It was three lines: "You are what you think. You become what you think. What you think becomes reality." Beneath the quote, she drew a row of flowers. That sign stayed on our mirror for years, and when it became destroyed by drops of water over time, she simply rewrote and reposted it. I remember a conversation driving home from our cabin at Sunday Lake. Like any parent, Mom presented what she believed as truth. Like any teenager, I challenged a lot of what my parents said. During that car drive, she told me that our minds could move mountains.

"Come on, Mom," I said, "do you really believe that?" We proceeded to have an absurd discussion about whether a mountain would move over time just because I believed it would. Poor Mom, and Dad too, for that matter. There was one year, probably not my parents' favorite, in which all five of us, their offspring, were teenagers. Aside from the moments of teenage resistance, Mom's messages about positive thinking and believing in ourselves did not fall on deaf ears. That night before the race, I knew that picturing myself breaking away from the other riders in various scenarios had just opened the door wider for me to actually do so the next day. Just as any disciple of my mom's teaching would, I visualized all sorts of positive scenarios before I fell asleep and likely dreamed more of the same.

Sitting through my public speaking class, SPCH 121, that next day, the Friday morning of the first women's Little 500 race day, I could barely stay focused on my classmates' presentations. Each student in our class was required to make a persuasive oral presentation to the class, and so for the last half of class, I listened to my classmates present "Ten Reasons You Should Get a Job at a Summer Camp" and "Why You Should Get a Liberal Arts Degree Instead of a Business Degree as an Undergrad." I tried to care about what they were saying, particularly because I would be giving my own speech the following week.

Instead, I envisioned my dad and sister on their car journey toward Bloomington. *They should be nearing Chicago right about now*, I thought. I considered restaurants to take them to if they managed to arrive early enough for lunch. I made a list of what I needed to bring to the track later. Then I drew a sketch of each item—two water bottles, team jacket, tape (to keep my shoelaces secured during the race), extra pair of shorts, etc. My legs bounced up and down under my desk. That day, my public speaking class, which lasted one hour and fifteen minutes, seemed to take twice as long. When we finally adjourned for the day, I rose and shot out of the classroom. Going to that class had been a test of my patience, as would be everything else on my schedule prior to four o'clock p.m. Eastern Standard Time, the moment I would be standing on the start line of the Little 500 race.

Kevin had decided that I would be the rider to start the race for our team. I was not sure why, but I thought it was maybe because I was forceful about maintaining my position in the pack. Or maybe it was because the first rider might do a longer shift or more laps overall, and I was sort of our endurance rider. We cyclists would start as a pack obviously, with all the teams lining up together and doing a few laps behind a pace car. Then Chappy Blackwell would wave the green flag and racing would begin. The men usually raced as a pack, taking advantage of the aerodynamics of riding through the wind together, for the entirety of their two-hundred-lap race.

No one really knew if the women would stay in a compact pack because of the wide variety of ability and fitness among the riders in that inaugural year. With the race being new for women, there were no true veteran riders, and essentially none of us, from any team, had much prior experience in racing a bike. Sure, I had competed in a few triathlons in high school, but I had done so without doing any specific or organized training for cycling—or running or swimming, for that matter. Women's cycling was a sport that most of us had neither seen nor heard of much.

The first-ever cycling event for women in any Olympic Games had occurred just a few years earlier in the 1984 Los Angeles games. I was fourteen years old then and watched a lot of the summer games that year. There was a lot of hype, and not only because they took place on American soil. The LA

Olympic Games were much anticipated because the United States, along with sixty-six other countries, had boycotted the previous Olympics, the Moscow games in 1976, to protest the Soviet invasion of Afghanistan. In the local press, there was also particular interest in one of the athletes who would compete in the first-ever Olympic cycling event for women. Connie Carpenter-Phinney had grown up in Madison, my hometown. She had already been to the Winter Olympics some years earlier and competed in speed skating. Now she was back, this time on the bike, and Wisconsin took pride in the homegrown athlete in the way that states do, claiming her as our own even though she had traded in Wisconsin for Colorado some years back.

Plus, McDonald's was supporting our athletes by giving out scratch-off promotional cards. An Olympic event was revealed when you scratched off the card. After the event listed on the card actually took place, you could take your card into McDonald's if Team USA had won a medal. At age fourteen, I apparently had no shame in elongating my walk home from school to stop by McDonald's and ask for scratch-off cards. Neither did my sister Molly. We loved Big Macs. We stopped by Mickey D's every day and built up supplies of the cards, maybe around forty each, thanks to the generosity of an employee who once handed us a large stack of cards. Molly and I eagerly awaited the Olympics and the events represented on our cards.

The LA games were a total boon, both for Team USA and for the Hellmuth girls. Each time Americans won a gold medal, the scratch-off card listing that event became redeemable for a Big Mac. If we won a silver, it was good for an order of large fries. And if Team USA took the bronze in the event listed, your scratch-off card would get you a Coke. Watching the Olympics had never been so fun. Americans won over eighty gold medals, over sixty silvers, and thirty bronze medals in the LA Olympics. My sister and I ate at McDonald's for lunch every day for weeks, turning in three cards each—a gold, bronze, and silver—to get ourselves a free lunch. Thank you, Ronald McDonald, for your generous contribution toward my teenage need for calories. I alone am to blame for lacking the self-control to space out my lunch visits and the subsequent acne breakout.

In 1984, Connie Carpenter-Phinney's Olympic gold medal win was memorable because she had won by inches. She had come toward the finish line in a breakaway of five riders. From that group, both she and her American teammate Rebecca Twig jumped ahead in the final sprint. Carpenter-Phinney performed a "bike throw" at the finish line, a move in which a rider shoves their bike forward to launch the front wheel in front of the competitor's wheel during a close finish. Throwing your bike can make the crucial difference between winning and losing. It took several minutes for the officials to declare Carpenter-Phinney the winner over Twig, who took the silver medal. In the first women's Olympic cycling race, just that one event, the two had matched the number of podium finishes earned by American men in the *entire* history of Olympic cycling competition. Inspired by the memory of the Olympic race, my Willkie Sprint teammates and I had practiced throwing our bikes forward ahead of adversaries too, just in case that skill came in handy at the finish of our race.

Walking back to the dorm from my speech class, I saw that Rob was aways ahead of me on the sidewalk. I hurried to catch him. Coming up on him, I could tell by how his hair was ruffled that he had probably awoken just in time to run off to class.

"Hey, let me guess," I said. "You had a late night partying with your buddy?" He confirmed that he had, and when he turned toward me, I could see it in his tired eyes as well. "Well done. I s'pose that is the responsibility of hosting. My dad and sister should be here in a few hours."

"You ready for the big race? I bought Jim a Willkie T-shirt," he said and unzipped his sweatshirt so I could see that he was already wearing his own Willkie tee. "He is psyched to see what Little 500 is all about. He actually did a little riding with me in high school."

"Aha. So you were one of the people who paid for my dinner last night," I said. "Our team dinner was covered by a last-minute round of T-shirt sales. Finally people decided to buy a few now that it's Little 500 weekend. Don't worry though, there are plenty left for you to buy as gifts for your brothers.

"I am already nervous. Nervous and excited," I said. "I just want to get to four o'clock. I am glad my dad and Ann are coming, but I feel like I'll be so distracted." I was excited to see them but did not want to lose focus or give my emotional energy to anything but the race that day.

"Do you want me to take them on a tour of campus?" said Rob. "I was going to take Jim around after lunch and show it to him. Assuming he's awake by then." Sleeping was always a central consideration for eighteen-year-olds. Rob's offer was a generous one, given the inherent stress of being presented with the father of your girlfriend for the first time. Since it did not make sense for my sister and Dad to drive out to their hotel in the boondocks and back before the race, I accepted.

"Are you sure you want to though?" I said. "Maybe you'd rather just hang out with your friend Jim." I considered for a moment how Rob and my dad might get along, and I figured that it would go well. Rob had accumulated a million factoids about the IU campus that I thought Dad would be interested in learning. Actually, they were probably a good match. I was excited for them to meet. I knew that my dad and sister would like Rob.

"Nah, Jim won't mind," he said. "He's pretty laid-back, and I haven't shown him much yet—except the HPER and Kirkwood Ave. He can come too." Of course Rob had taken Jim to the HPER. To the courts. The HPER was the recreation center located in the heart of campus right across from the Memorial Union. It was a big facility with a weight room, cardio areas, some gyms and exercise studios, a swimming pool, and a diving well. But the most impressive part was the big fieldhouse area, where there were ten (no kidding, ten!) full regulation-size basketball courts. More impressive than having ten courts was the fact that they were always full. I had heard about the sport of basketball being like a religion in Indiana. From around four o'clock until eleven p.m. every day, there was open court time and you could witness the worshippers of the sport. Consistently there were pick-up games going on at pretty much every level. Karen and I went occasionally to the HPER just to get out of the dorm. Running on the track around the ten courts, observing those hotly contested games, I learned what basketball meant to those who grew up Hoosier. Everything. Which was the same way I felt about the Little 500 that year.

Back at the dorm, Rob and I went to the bike room. In the hallway outside, we found Kristin and Kevin just leaving. They were loading up bikes and wind trainers to take to our pit at the track. The first thing I saw upon entering the room were our four helmets lined up in a row.

"Wait, when did this happen?" I said. The helmets had been freshly painted, and they were a sight of beauty. Robin's-egg blue, they were the exact color of the blue lettering on our yellow race jerseys. In yellow, across the front, was written "Willkie." Also in yellow, a racing stripe was painted down the middle, and our pit number "8" was painted on both sides and the back of the helmet. They looked very sharp and perfectly mimicked the clean detail of the Indy 500 race cars. They were a perfect match with our jerseys to complete our race-day outfit. Rob and I picked up the helmets and marveled at them. Something swelled inside of me, which I identified as either pride for all the hard miles put in to arrive at that day or appreciation of Kristin, who was surely the artist behind the marvelous paint job. Probably both.

I ran out to the car where Kristin and Kevin were loading the bikes and trainers.

"You did that? You painted the helmets, right?" I said to Kristin, who smiled at the recognition and my clear approval of her race-day surprise. I gave her a squeeze. "They look awesome!"

"We had some paint left over after finishing the pit boards," she said. "They turned out even better than I thought they would." We would be the only team that day with stylized helmets announcing our team name and pit number and sporting our team colors. It gave us an important mental boost on a day when we needed one.

I had packed and rechecked my bag for the track twice by the time my dad and sister arrived. The big windows of our room faced the parking lot behind the dorm. I was looking down, keeping an eye out for their arrival as I did some stretching. When the familiar VW Rabbit did show up, I ran down to meet them. I was so far from home, the drive taking nearly seven hours depending on Chicago traffic, that I had not gone home since Christmas break. I had seen Ann a month earlier in Las Vegas, but I had essentially soldiered through my freshman year with no trips home except at Thanksgiving and Christmas.

"I am so happy you guys are here," I said, feeling the warmth inside that came only from being with those who knew and loved me best. I collected and gave out bear hugs to Dad and Ann as they stretched their legs after the long drive.

"Come on, let's get out of the parking lot. Ann's never seen my room. You have to meet Karen too, sister. You'll love my roommate." My sister had a cognitive disability and had not gone to college so was curious to see where I had been all year. She was also a champion Special Olympian, so I knew she would love the race. We sat around my room chatting for a while. Karen was there with her boyfriend, Ron. She put my hair up in a French braid while we chatted, so it would be out of my face during the race.

"We can all go to the race together," Karen said to my dad. "Kerry has to go meet her team at the stadium earlier, so you can come with us." I had orchestrated plans for Dad and Ann during the few hours when I would ride to the track to meet my team and warm up and do race preparation. They would do a campus tour with Rob and then make their way over to Bill Armstrong Stadium with Karen.

Rob showed up, and I introduced him to my dad and sister. I might have been more worried about the moment of introducing him to my dad—he was one of my first boyfriends and the first I had ever presented to my dad—but my capacity for nervousness was all taken up by the looming race. Anyway, Rob had cleaned himself up and lost the just-rolled-out-of-bed look that he had had earlier. In my opinion, he was charming. I figured my dad could not help but like him.

Fathers always represent towering, important figures. My dad was actually literally towering at six feet, four inches. Rob seemed small standing next to him. As Dad, Ann, Rob, and Jim headed off together, I mouthed an emphatic "Thank you" to Rob. In the presence of my dad though, we did not touch or kiss goodbye. I hoped that their campus tour would go well and trusted that it would. I sent them off and turned my attention, finally, to the race.

I got dressed in my cycling gear, donning the yellow jersey. Sizing seemed to be based, as was everything that inaugural year, on the men's event. The yellow jersey was quite baggy, even on me, one of the larger women in the race. But at that moment, the detail of its excessive size seemed unimportant to me. Used to wearing T-shirts at the track, I was not too concerned with the aerodynamics of tight-fitting cycling-designed clothing. It felt important just to be wearing a cycling jersey.

I felt a shimmer of excitement as I dressed myself in the crisp, new, bright yellow jersey. I looked in the mirror. Delta Faucet was the sponsor of the entire women's race, and their logo was emblazoned across the chest of the jersey. "Willkie Sprint" and the big number 8 were on the back. The sleeves were loose on my thin upper arms, and I made the decision to roll them up. Yes, that was better. I ran kitty-corner across the hall to Louise's room and knocked. No answer, but she came down the hall from the bathroom, not yet dressed in cycling gear.

"Look at you!" she said. "I was just going to get dressed too. Wow! So official."

"Wait till you see our helmets," I said and told her about the paint job that rendered them sparkling and new. "They look so cool."

"So does our jersey," said Louise. "I am already nervous. I keep thinking that I have to pee. I have gone down there like ten times." She motioned toward the bathrooms.

"By the way, I *like* the rolled sleeves," she said. "Very sexy." I laughed out loud.

"The sleeves are gaping and baggy, so I thought that would annoy me," I said. "I wasn't really going for sexy." When Louise had dressed a few minutes later and we were heading out, I said, "Roll your sleeves, or they will function as a sail during the race. See what I mean?"

"No, I'm good," said Louise. "Trust me, only you can pull off making functionality look cool." She laughed. I was pretty sure that, like Kirsten's comparing me to Dave Stohler, this could be another compliment that was not a compliment. I shrugged and kept my sleeves rolled as we headed off to meet our team.

The scene at Bill Armstrong Stadium that day was nothing we had ever witnessed in our daily sessions there over the past few months. It was bustling with activity. The large signs at the turnoff for the track had big bunches of balloons attached to them. The parking lot, which generally had just a handful of cars, was already full. The stadium seemed decorated for a giant party. The mechanics' room below the north-side stands was full of activity. Teams were picking up their race bikes. We parked our townie bikes and set off toward our pit. The entrance gate that had been open all season was now only open to athletes and teams. Spectators had to use the separate official entrance gate, where they had to purchase or show their race tickets.

The track looked amazing. The pit boards were up all around the track, so the entire interior was lined with bright colors. The chain-link fence was now obscured, in favor of the brightly painted boards. Five red convertibles were parked on the infield. A circus tent had been erected on the infield at the far end of the track, apparently to host journalists. It had no side walls, allowing visibility of the track for teams on the backstretch. News teams and reporters milled around on the infield, some with big cameras around their necks or video cameras set up on tripods. The infield had a stage set up with some shiny trophies displayed on a table.

"*There* you are," Kevin said to Louise and me as we arrived at our pit. Kevin was wearing a pink oxford. I had been mourning the loss of his mom all week, and his gesture in her memory touched me. On the list of reasons why

I wanted to win the race was to honor her, or I guess rather to honor Kevin for what he had gone through, for his dedication to our little team in spite of living through one of the hardest moments of his life as he coached us that semester. Kristin was also wearing a bright pink polo shirt in solidarity with her co-coach. Kirsten, Amy, and Wes, who was our official mechanic for race day, were already there as well. In front of our pit boards, two bikes on trainers were set up for us to warm up and warm down during the race. Kevin was allowed to stay in the pit with us, but at race time, Kristin as assistant coach had to be on the other side of the fence. Wes would spend much of the race on the infield just across from our pit with our spare bike, ready to take off for any corner of the track if we were involved in a wreck. Kristin eventually took the spot front and center behind us where she could literally reach over and give us a pat of encouragement. For all of us, it was as if Kristin was with us—in the pit and on the bike. She was so one-of-us that it did not matter which side of the fence she was standing on.

"One arm straight up?" Kevin said. He wanted us to review his arm gestures and what they meant.

"Means to come in for an exchange in one lap," I said, answering quickly as if in a game show quiz where the speed of your response mattered. I was already in competition mode.

"One arm out to the side?" he continued.

"It's going to be a one-bike exchange," Amy said. "Kevin, don't worry. We know the signals." She smiled at him and patted him on the back.

Warm-ups started, and we were happy to find that the track had been well prepared for the big day. It was nicely packed down, likely having been given prime treatment the past day or two. Usually the track was maintained by watering it down at night. That way, it would harden a bit as it dried. Later it would be raked. By the end of the daily track practices, spanning five hours, the track was usually cruddy and rutted. It was maybe just my own excitement about the race, but I thought, *Boy, does this track feel fast today.* At least for the start of the race, the track's cinder surface would remain well packed and fast underneath us. We ran through some exchanges and then did some efforts to get our heart rates up, and our muscles opened up for racing. But not too many. We wanted to save it all for the race.

Hoopla prior to the race start was to be expected, but we had not anticipated the crowds. People, fans who were mostly students but also family members and locals, were entering the stadium in what seemed to be an unending stream. I heard a sharp whistle I recognized as Rob's. I found him in the stands and smiled. He responded with his own smile and a two-eyed blink. The fans settled, for the most part, in the permanent stands along the front straightaway where the start/finish line was. As those stands started filling up, we looked at one another with a bit of surprise. That previous fall, I had attended a soccer game in the same stadium, but there was a relatively dismal turnout, despite the soccer team being a contender for the NCAA championship. The inaugural women's Little 500 race was drawing way more spectators.

Aside from the main stands filling, cheering for teams with pits on the backstretch like ours drew fans to the temporary bleachers that had been erected over the past month. Our friends and family were either in those bleachers or stood along the fence directly behind us. Karen arrived with my dad and sister. They crowded on the other side of the pit boards with our other supporters. Ann has always enjoyed festive atmospheres, and she was excited, yelling, "Good luck, sister!" to me multiple times. Eventually, she planted herself front and center behind our pit, with the stronger-than-Wisconsin sun hitting her directly in the face. Over the next hour or so, in a strong display of sisterly love, she proceeded to get a blazing sunburn, the kind where you could see the precise outline of her sunglasses the next day, and to lose her voice while cheering her lungs out for me and my teammates.

There was pomp and ceremony, as if the bigness of the party could make up for waiting patiently on the sidelines for thirty-seven years before being granted our own race. The next day at the men's race, I learned that the high degree of ceremony was simply an integral part of the World's Greatest College Weekend tradition. Many of IU's leaders, including the chancellor, Herman B Wells, were in attendance and milling around on the infield. The number of photographers and press members was shocking. They were all present to watch us race.

The riders were called to the start area to line up by team, all four riders standing together. I heard Dad yell out, "Go get 'em, hon!" and I turned to wave to him as we headed to the start line.

Phyllis Klotman, the dean of women's affairs who had helped make the women's edition of the race a reality, addressed all the athletes and the crowd. She put things in historical perspective. A Mini 500 trike had been brought

to the track for her to take a symbolic ride on it before telling us something
to the effect of, "No longer are the women of Indiana University relegated to
riding a trike. It took too long in the making, but, as of today, if *all you want
is to ride your bicycle* in the Little 500, you can." Phyllis Klotman raised her
small fist for emphasis. A cheer went up from riders and fans alike. Given
that age is relative, the tiny dean seemed ancient to me at my young eighteen
years. She was probably in her sixties; I tried to estimate her age to figure out
whether she had actually just made reference to Queen's song *Bicycle Race* ("I
want to ride my bicycle") intentionally or not.

"I want to ride my bicycle," said Louise, singing the famous refrain softly
under her breath. "I want to ride my bike."

"Me too," I said and smiled back at her.

The members of each team were introduced as we walked an entire parade
lap of the track. Thirty teams had survived the long march toward race day.
We had lost three riders to broken collarbones, one team had dropped out,
and several others had struggled to arrive with four committed and healthy
riders on race day. Fans got rowdy as their teams passed, including our own
fans when we passed them on the backstretch.

Next, the longtime master of ceremonies for the men's Little 500 race,
Chappy Blackwell, explained some rules to the athletes and the crowd. He
showed us an area where a white penalty box had been drawn in chalk near
the start/finish line and indicated that penalties had to be served within ten
laps of when they were announced. I cringed at the thought and prayed we
did not get one. Penalties were issued as a specific number of seconds and
served by one team member riding into the penalty box and standing still
next to her bike for that number of seconds. Teams were given penalties
for things like illegal exchanges, impeding another team, unsportsmanlike
conduct, and "creeping," which meant advancing on the lead team under the
yellow flag.

Acting as chief steward for the women's inaugural Little 500 race, Chappy
Blackwell went on to explain the significance of each flag. We would start
the race shortly with the waving of the green flag. But there were others: the
yellow flag came out if there was a wreck that they were trying to clear from
the track or athletes down for a period of time and meant "ride with caution
and maintain your position relative to the leader"; the red flag was rare but

meant "stop riding and maintain your position until further notice is given"; the white flag was waved when the winning team was starting its final lap; and the checkered flag, well, a big cheer erupted when Chappy announced, "The checkered flag, that one needs no explanation."

For a moment, I pictured my dad listening to the rules. I knew already that he would eventually tire of standing and amble up to a seat in the stands behind him before the race's end. You come to know exactly what your parents will say or do in almost any situation, and I could almost hear him saying, "This is really neat! Just like the Indy 500, Ann, you hear that?" My entire sporting childhood, my parents had rarely missed a meet, game, or race. It was no surprise that my dad had come, seven-hour drive or not. I was happy that he and my sister were in the crowd.

Finally, the teams were asked to return to the pits, leaving behind only their starting riders. That was me.

"You know what to do," Kirsten said, patting my shoulder as she headed back to the pit.

"Yeah, just stay away from everyone else," Amy said, kidding but also serious. We were wary of crashes—for which the Little 500 is well known. We had certainly witnessed plenty of them in practice.

I gave my teammates a salute, and the starting athletes from each team were arranged in the three-by-eleven grid. I looked forward and spotted the Thetas' starting rider. She would start in the coveted pole position. Fitting for one of the founding mothers of the Little 500 race.

"Hey," I called out, and when she turned, "Good luck!"

She offered me the same, referring to me as "Stretch," a nickname for me in the Theta pit. I considered why this was what they called me—the long legs, I supposed, and maybe the long everything. Everyone's height seems double when they are splayed out during exchanges. I decided to take the fact that they had a nickname for me as a compliment rather than an offense. It fit with the camaraderie and jesting at the track. All of us had been poking fun at one another for months.

We were to complete three laps in the three-by-eleven formation before the start of the one-hundred-lap race. Following the string of red 1988 Pontiac Sunbird convertibles holding important people such as top IU athletes, race sponsors, and university royalty, we would complete the first two laps, including a photo lap in which pictures could be taken with the riders in the moment of calm before the storm of racing, and a warm-up lap during which all the convertibles except the pace car itself would exit the track. Finally, the pace car would lead us through the pace lap, steadily increasing speed until it sped off, at which point we would pass the start line, where Chappy Blackwell would stand waving the green flag. The race would officially begin when we passed him.

CHAPTER

"LADIES, MOUNT YOUR Roadmaster bicycles!" As grand marshal, Phyllis Klotman delivered the cherished command that signaled the start of the women's inaugural Little 500 race. It had been adapted from the traditional phrase issued to start the men's race over the past thirty-seven years—replacing "gentlemen" with "ladies." It was met with a rousing cheer and the release of what seemed to be a hundred balloons from the infield. It was the moment launching the show that everyone was gathered to watch, the race that had been years in the making.

As the eighth qualifier, our starting spot was located in the center of the third row, right in between riders from the Notorious and Kappa Delta teams. I wished them both good luck in the race as we each mounted our bicycles. I was happy to be starting in front of over twenty teams. Once the race started, I planned to settle into the second row of riders, getting a free ride in the draft of the first-row riders. Staying up front would help me avoid crashes caused by jockeying for position mid-pack. I figured that I would get through the first few laps before looking for opportunities to start our effort of lapping the pack, toward the end of my shift.

The mood shifted in the pack during the pace lap. The pace car took us through the second turn before it accelerated and raced ahead of us, past the start line, and exited from the track. We passed Chappy Blackwell ceremoniously waving the green flag. We were off!

The roar of the crowd replaced that of the pace car's accelerating engine. The noise reminded me of the IU football games, thousands of college students screaming their lungs out. I later found out that it was truly thousands. The total number in attendance at the inaugural women's Little 500 was, in fact, reported to be over fifteen thousand spectators. The turnout wildly exceeded expectations and fully confirmed the validity of the women's edition. It was a rowdy crowd to boot. After months of practicing at the track with no crowds, the sheer volume was amazing.

Apparently I was not the only one motivated by the cheering. Instantly, my fellow riders swarmed up and into position on both sides of me. The race started fast, but I felt like a diesel engine—not yet up to speed. It took me a nervous lap or two to get my rhythm. What a relief when I felt my legs kick in. Cyclists say that if you are not moving forward in the pack, then you are moving backward. By the time I was running all systems full gas, my lethargic start had left me buried in the middle of the fourth row, not where I had wanted to be. I worked my way over to the outside of the pack and started moving forward. Riding on the outside made for easier mobility since I was no longer locked in. It also meant that I had more ground to cover than those on the innermost lane. I decided to move up and take the inside lane. I could see the Theta and Alpha Phi riders leading the race. I needed to be closer to them.

At the end of lap 4, as we were heading down the front stretch, a rider to my left suddenly swerved so close to me that our handlebars started to lock. Simultaneously, I heard screams and the undeniable sound of bicycles crashing. Never a sound you wanted to hear. I shoved down my instinct to panic and tried to stay relaxed as I straightened up, calmly detached myself from the rider leaning against me, and started to move forward.

The sound of that crash behind me was all I needed to hightail it straight to the front of the pack, which is where I found myself within one half lap.

First I led the pack alongside the Theta rider, who had been leading the pack essentially since the race began. Then I was solo leading the pack.

As a result of the crash, the yellow flag was displayed as riders scrambled to get back on their bikes and mechanics hurried to bring new bikes to the scene. The yellow flag meant all teams had to slow down and maintain their positions relative to the lead rider, which at that point was me. Normally I shunned taking the lead because I liked tucking into the wind-protected pack. Hearing that crash though and having that rider's handlebars hook onto mine, I decided to put a premium on staying clear of others entirely. It simply was not worth risking a crash.

We rode several laps under the yellow flag. I stayed up front, within the first couple of riders. As suddenly as it arrived, the yellow was gone and we were back under the green flag and normal racing conditions. On the tenth lap of the race, Kevin signaled that I would be doing an exchange. I wanted to leave a nice-sized gap before I got off the bike, to make sure we stayed at the front. Thus I took a long flyer off the front, for three-quarters of a lap, before coming out to exchange to Louise. With the resulting gap, I figured Louise would have plenty of time to hop right back into the lead of the race.

The exchange did not go well. My speed was faster than hers, and we did not equalize our speed before I released the bike. She grabbed at the bike, which swerved and fell. She moved as quickly as she could to pick it up and get moving again. I had tried to give her a sizable gap so she wouldn't have to enter at the rear and fight her way back up through the pack. In the end, the gap served another purpose. She had more time to pick up the bike and make up the time lost on our botched exchange. She was passed by the loose, strung-out pack of riders but chased fervently to catch back up.

"Looks like the Willkie Sprint rider is struggling to get back to the pack," said the booming voice of the announcer. Louise later told me that she heard this announcement and it angered and embarrassed her. While she felt that her reentry to the pack was guaranteed—she could see the tail end of the peloton getting closer—this announcement lit a fire under her. Usually cyclists ride in a tight pack, called a *peloton*. The word is derived from French, and it also means "small ball," which is how a compact peloton looks traveling around the track. Louise not only powered back into the peloton but also worked up the outside of the peloton over the next few laps until she tucked into the first spot behind the leader.

"Perfect, Louise," I heard Kevin say to himself. From that point on, she stayed in the sweet spot of the peloton, riding up front in the second row of cyclists. There she could both conserve energy by drafting and stay out of danger.

That, in a few words, is the biggest factor in making decisions in a bike race. Any cyclist riding in a race is constantly seeking to conserve energy for the final sprint. The best way to conserve energy is to use less of it by riding in the draft of another rider. I had learned about the benefits of drafting from an article in a cycling magazine. Wind tunnel testing on aerodynamics had demonstrated that riders who were well-positioned could reduce anywhere from 27 percent to 50 percent of the wind resistance involved in moving forward, depending on variables like the size and bike positioning of the lead rider, how closely the drafting rider follows the lead rider's wheel, and the direction of the wind. The drag reduction translates to a huge amount of energy saved. Of course, the amount of energy saved is relative to how much wind exists and to the speed being traveled. The faster you are moving and the stronger the headwind is, the more you benefit from drafting.

The only moment that matters is your position at the end of the race, so it makes sense to conserve energy to the utmost degree possible until that moment. Our race was a bit more complicated because the Little 500 was a sort of relay race. We wanted to conserve energy, yes, but only one of us would need to conserve it until the end of the race. The other three teammates could burn their energy during the earlier laps. In fact, that was actually the point. You wanted all your energy, everything you had to give, left on the track that day.

Kirsten or Amy would finish the race for our team. They were our two most powerful sprinters. Louise was wise to conserve her energy by drafting but also to stay up toward the front. A peloton is a thing of beauty, both extrinsically, its bright colors melding together, and intrinsically, with its aerodynamic efficiency. It's also very dangerous. Because you are riding just inches from others on all four sides, you have to be constantly watching for erratic moves by others. Unsteady riders cause crashes, which can be unavoidable if they set off a chain reaction in front of you. That's why the safest position in a peloton is up front. The first row does not have the benefit of someone cutting their wind drag. The second row is about the best spot you can be in. And that's where Louise had settled in. I was relieved to see her come around in that position lap after lap.

After six laps or so, Kevin signaled for Louise to come out. Kirsten was up next on the bike. Louise came in and nailed a solid exchange with Kirsten. We were at lap 18. As she settled on a bike trainer to warm-down her legs, Louise rejoiced that she had managed to regain the sweet spot of the peloton despite her shaky exchange with me.

"Nice job!" I said. Her second exchange, the one with Kirsten involving two bikes, had gone well. She had struggled with exchanging for months, and she was visibly relieved that her initial stint on the bike had gone well enough. We high-fived and watched Kirsten come around in second place, behind one rider at the start of a long string of riders.

The peloton was dissolving. Eight teams had gone down in the crash at lap 4, when I had been on the bike. Most of them had lost enough time getting untangled from the wreck or exchanging their bike or rider that they were trailing behind and unable to catch back on. The fast pace of the race had led to the other twenty-plus teams being strung out in a long line, then separating as riders could not hold the pace. Others had made slow exchanges and were unable to get back on the rear of the pack. The peloton had dwindled to around ten teams, not very tight-knit at all, followed by solo riders or groups of two or three working together.

Next to go in was Amy. As she warmed up on one of the bike trainers, she seemed jittery and nervous. Kirsten came in smoothly to Amy's right for the two-bike exchange and managed to stop on the line as Amy sprinted off. Yay, we had pulled off another strong exchange. Each exchange that was completed well was a small victory.

I could see by the way that Amy grabbed the bike from Kirsten and sprinted off that she was on a mission. And when Amy turned on her steely resolve . . . well, watch out! We were at lap 23. Amy easily reentered the front group. After one lap, two of the teams with her went out for exchanges. Amy seized the opportunity. She sprinted and pulled away. Neither the entering Theta rider, nor the cyclist from the Notorious team were able to regain her wheel.

"There she goes," said Kirsten. "Look at her!" Amy had taken the lead of the race, and she was catching and passing anyone in her path. More importantly, she had opened up a nice-sized gap between herself and the other riders who were on the same lap as us. She was solo. Our fans behind the pit yelled bloody murder as Amy approached, coming through the second corner.

"One, two, three, four, five," I said as Amy raced past our pit, counting out the time from when she passed until the next rider did. "She's got a five-second gap." A prickling feeling of nervousness coursed through me. I felt my heart speed up. I did not know if we could make it last, but Amy had opened a gap. She was adding to it with every pedal stroke.

"Amy's on fire," Kirsten shouted to me over the crowd noise. Kevin told me to get warmed up. He was serious, 100 percent focused under the pressure. I hopped on a trainer and opened up the blood flow in my legs with some high rpm spinning. All of our eyes were glued on Amy's bold riding.

"Nine seconds," called out Kirsten. We were measuring our lead, counting the seconds between her and the next rider, who happened to be the Theta rider. Was Amy on a mission to lap the pack? She was definitely putting in her all by the look on her face. But was it too early in the race to break away and be able to sustain it throughout the entire race? I steeled my determination right then and vowed I would not be caught, not on my watch. I would fight with everything I had to hold our lead. *If anything*, I told myself, *I will increase our lead*. It was positive self-talk. I reinforced my own intention with those words. I envisioned myself increasing our lead even more.

"Here she comes," said Kirsten. Instead of counting this time, she shouted, "Come on, Amy!" Louise had her hands together as if . . . Was she praying? She leaned forward and shouted a long "Go-o-o" as Amy came by. I counted out around eleven seconds, but by the time she reached the finish line, she had added another.

"Team Willkie Sprint is now leading the race by twelve seconds," came the announcement over the loudspeaker. Amy whizzed past again, to enormous cheering by our fans. Louise and Kirsten leaned forward from the pit and shouted out, as did I from the bike trainer, where I kept my legs moving.

Kevin was concentrating on when to bring Amy in. There was a signal we were supposed to send him if we were getting tired and wanted to come out. I knew that none of us would give that signal, two fingers extended down from our grip on the handlebars, unless we were in horrible shape, absolutely bonking. Kevin was thus fully responsible for orchestrating the length of our pulls. He bent his knees and squatted down, bringing his face to the cyclists' eye level when we passed. He was studying us for signs that it was time.

Next lap, Kirsten and Louise stood next to my trainer, and we counted the distance between Amy and the three riders who were working together behind her.

"Nine, ten, eleven, twelve, thirteen, fourteen, fifteen, sixteen, seventeen, *eighteen!*" We squealed at the strong lead. I heard Kristin shouting for Amy from behind us. I turned and smiled at her. We exchanged expressions of fear, joy, hope, excitement, and about one hundred other emotions wrapped together in one. Since Kevin had signaled Amy to come out on the next lap, he signaled for me to hop off the bike trainer. I looked at the neighboring pits to see if anyone else was exchanging and did not see anyone stepping forward.

"You feeling OK? Ready?" Kevin asked. I was. Nervousness had been present in every cell of my body a few minutes earlier. Now though, as the moment to reenter the race approached, a feeling of strength and calm came over me. I was ready to go. I got in position.

"We have got more than a twenty-second lead," Kirsten called out to me. I nodded and felt my game face take over my expression.

"You can do this, Kerr," said Kristin loudly from the fence, almost in a matter-of-fact tone.

"Exchange coming in," I shouted toward the pits prior to ours. We issued that courtesy call to make sure people stayed clear. I stood ready to sprint, looking back over my shoulder as Amy swung out from the inside of corner two. I started running and felt automatic-pilot kick in as we executed a solid exchange. After swinging my legs down onto the pedals as my bum landed on the bike seat, I stood and sprinted with all my might to maintain the lead that Amy had worked so hard for.

Let's go, I said to myself, already breathing hard from the initial effort, *let's go, let's go. Smooth. Fast.* Rather than focus on my lungs, which seemed to be exploding, I thought about my legs and pictured them turning over faster and faster.

"Unofficially, it looks like team eight has opened up quite a gap on the pack," I heard the announcer say. And a lap later: "Here comes Willkie; let's cheer her on. She's opened up a nice gap." Hearing about the gap was reassuring since I obviously did not see anything behind me.

"If Dave Blase could see this," the announcer said, referring to the real Phi Kappa Psi rider whom the movie character Dave Stohler was based on. "Willkie Sprint has a twenty-three-second gap with thirty laps completed." Great.

When I had exited the race earlier, I knew that there was an intact peloton behind me, minus a few teams who had crashed in the fourth lap. But now, the neat peloton of cyclists had been blown apart. I was passing lapped teams. It felt like chaos, like each rider for herself, basically like track practice.

For the fans' benefit, the teams were tracked on a large scoreboard each time they passed the start/finish line. There, the lap counters, one per team, turned over big numbers to reflect the current lap number of each team. While that might help fans, it was not really used by the teams themselves; each knew where they were relative to the leader.

I only knew that all the teams were trying to chase *me* down. That was enough. Quickly I got myself into a decent rhythm. To keep my speed up, I focused on riders in front of me as motivation, trying to catch and blow by them. After I passed one, I would set my sights on the next. I smiled. It was like playing a live version of the popular arcade video game Atari's *Pole Position*, my second favorite after *Ms. Pac-Man*.

Each time I approached my pit, I looked to see if Kevin was making a gesture. My teammates yelled things I could not hear. Kevin leaned forward and stared straight into my eyes each time I passed. He moved his hands in circles over one another, index fingers pointed in, imitating the pedaling motion. He never said a word, probably understanding that I would not hear him anyway with the noise of the crowds.

Four or five laps into my stint, I noticed his pink shirt. I felt a surge of motivation to win the Little 500 for him. For his mom. He really believed in us. He believed that we *could* win. To my own conviction, I added Kevin's conviction. I felt faster. If he'd had a great *Leave It to Beaver* childhood, it was in large part because of his mom. She was there with us, present in her son and his pink shirt, and looking down on him. She believed in him. I added his mom's conviction to my own. I felt stronger.

Thinking about his mom brought up a vision of my own mom. I could hear her standard cheer, "Go, KK! Go get 'em!" from the million soccer games, swim meets, and other races where she had shouted that out to me, using our family's nickname for me. She was not at the race but wished she was. I added her ever-present confidence in me to my own conviction. I felt faster.

I saw Amy yelling words I could not pick out from the crowd noise. I thought of her strong riding to get us this advantage. I remembered her saying her mom was her best friend. I added Amy's conviction, and her mom's, to my effort. I felt faster. I thought of Louise's mom reaching toward her from behind the pit boards on the other side of the fence. I had met her before the race. She had driven in from Kentucky. She told me about being in the Kappa Alpha Theta sorority when she was back in college—but promised not to cheer for the Thetas during the race. I thought of Louise's "secret training" rides with me and how she had toiled away on her bike all year. I added Louise's conviction, and her mom's, to my own. I felt stronger.

Then I added Kirsten's conviction, how hard she worked at everything, to my effort. I felt faster. Then Kristin. Cheering right that moment in her bright pink polo shirt, she had been a constant presence supporting us all throughout the year. She truly believed in us. I felt faster. Carrying all of the support and conviction of our little team with me, I felt as strong as ever. I rode six blazing laps. I gathered up the intention of everyone who was cheering for us and added it to my own. I funneled all of it—the support, positivity, and belief in us—into a feeling of strength that carried me like a strong tailwind.

When I came out for an exchange with Kirsten, we led the race by nearly half a lap. I had maintained the lead that Amy had gained for us, even added to it. We did a two-bike exchange. Coming in fast, I barely stopped in time. My feet skidded to a stop right before the line, and I had to lift the bike off the ground to keep it from crossing the line. I swung the bike to a stop on the other side of my body. I checked on Kirsten and saw that she had already settled into a fast pace. She leaned low over the bike, minimizing the air resistance. I made sure no one was arriving for an exchange and turned to head back into our pit, which I found bubbling with tense emotion. It was even stronger than the palpable hope at our table the night before, because here we were, doing it. We had a long way to go. The race was only nearing the halfway mark. Anything could happen. But still, we were leading the race by a half lap. We had them all on the run. *Don't be afraid to win.* I dared to believe.

12

CHAPTER

"LOUISE, GET WARMED UP," Kevin said. Kirsten was moving fast and holding the lead well. Two laps into Kirsten's stint, a fresh rider reentered the race for the Thetas. With rested legs, she made up some ground on us. It was not much, but it made us nervous. The race had become a chase of our team, led by the Thetas but including the Delta Delta Delta team, Kappa Delta, Notorious, and the Stonies.

Kevin decided right then to scrap his original plan for the race, which was essentially based on having us ride longer turns to avoid potential time lost on exchanges. The race was moving at a much faster speed than anyone expected. He thought it was in our best interest to keep the speed high. He made an adjustment to his strategy, having us ride shorter stints on the bike. Our exchanges were reliable, and nothing was better than fresh legs. Kirsten rode only three laps before Kevin pulled her out and Louise went in for the same short stint. Kevin still varied the number of laps we each rode, based on what he knew of our riding and what he saw happening live. Amy was displaying the same powerful riding that she had shown early on in the race when she got our precious lead.

Around lap 40, we had a big scare. Louise came in and exchanged the bike to Amy. The strong rider on the Theta bike had been putting in a monster effort to catch Louise. Our exchange allowed their rider to come so close to catching Amy as she was reentering from the exchange that the announcer said, "Looks like they're caught!" He corrected himself in the next breath: "Or close anyway." We watched tensely as Amy sprinted back up to speed after the exchange. With her powerful riding, she was able to shoot ahead and once again increase the gap between us and the chasing Theta rider. Phew.

"They were almost caught," said the announcer. "If you can close that gap, then . . . it's a bike race." The Theta rider had come very close to doing just that.

Along with chasing riders from other teams, the Thetas had been making some valiant efforts and long turns on the bike. Their strong riding might reel us in closer, bring them within one-quarter of a lap or even closer to our rider, but they struggled to catch us. The high pace helped us. The stronger chasers from the ten or so teams who were on the same lap as us would eventually become exhausted or suffer from lactic acid buildup. Inevitably they would slow down or go out for an exchange. We managed to fend off the chasers with Kevin's strategy for short exchanges and a high pace. Riders from other teams seemed to stay on the bike for longer sets of laps. Two of the Thetas were among the strongest riders chasing us—the ones who seemed capable of reeling us in, maybe. Or maybe not.

After five laps, Amy exchanged the bike to me, and then I exchanged back to her after five laps. All four of us were rotating through, giving it our all, but Kevin worked Amy and me particularly hard throughout the long middle of the race. He seemed to be keeping Kirsten more rested, probably already thinking of having a sprinter ready for the finish.

Following the close call around lap 40, we maintained a lead that wavered but stayed consistently between one-quarter to one-half lap. The Thetas, Notorious, Sigma Kappa, Tri-Delts, and Alpha Epsilon Pi were chasing. Sometimes these teams were working together, but often they were solo due to timing their exchanges disparately with each other.

"We don't have a lot of wind-breaking—when you've got a pack and you can get a break from the wind. They're all out here riding into the wind on their own," said the announcer just after lap 50, the halfway point of the race. His thundering announcements both animated and kept the crowd informed throughout the race. He suggested that the chasing teams might want to pool their efforts together.

In our pit, we had stopped counting seconds long ago. We were just following the race, intently. We twisted our heads back and forth between our rider and the chasers. We used the landmarks of the track to determine whether they were gaining or losing ground on us. Each lap in which we kept our solid lead was a small victory. But it was, of course, the big victory that we wanted. The strategy of lapping the pack had become somewhat meaningless when the peloton fell apart. Our goal had become to stay out in front. We collectively turned our fierce determination toward staving off the chasers. And we believed.

From lap 50 through lap 80, we just fought to keep our lead. Kevin originally planned on Amy being on the bike at the end of the race. But he had already demonstrated fluidity and flexibility with his plan, scrapping it, for example, to shorten our turns on the bike and keep our pace high. Longer pulls would have made more sense if we were able to hide out in a peloton, taking advantage of drafting. Maintaining a solo breakaway was more exhausting. Our shortened stints on the bike accommodated fighting alone at the front of the race and working to keep ourselves there. On the run, our goal became *staying* on the run. We rode our hearts out, hoping to ride into history. Luckily we had seamless exchanges and solid efforts with churning legs.

Realizing the crucial moment and the need to keep our speed high in order not to be caught in the waning laps of the race, Kevin had us do a series of even shorter stints on the bike. I had done the last longer stint on the bike, seven laps from lap 75 to 82, when Kirsten took over and rode just three laps until lap 85, followed by Louise, who also rode three laps until lap 88, and Amy, who rode four laps.

As Amy rode away, we watched her recede down the straightaway and then turned our heads to see the Theta rider arriving. Something was wrong. She had a pained expression and tossed the bike down upon arriving at her pit. She was coming in for an exchange. But it seemed that no one was ready and waiting. *What was going on*, we wondered. I felt a pang of sympathy for the Theta rider, who had been riding so strongly throughout the race. It looked like she was experiencing leg cramps and had come in early, unexpectedly.

It was unclear whether any teammate was ready to enter the race. One did react quickly—grabbing a bike and sprinting off—but still it seemed they had a slower exchange.

I hated to see them in difficulty. The Theta riders had maintained a hero-like quality for me since the dreary fall day in Dunn Meadow when I had first heard of their qualification attempt the previous year. They had brought the women's Little 500 race to life. They were also really cool. From my freshman perspective, the story of their feat made them role models for me, for everyone really. The riders at the track looked up to them in general. I had watched them being interviewed that morning by a news camera. They were all smiles at the living proof that the women's Little 500 race was a big hit: the crowds had been pouring in, the teams warming up, and the stands filling up. Success had already been achieved for them before the race even began. Winning it would be the icing on the cake, but they already had reason to be tremendously satisfied.

On lap 92, it was our turn for leg pain. Amy came out cramping badly. I found this out much later though, because I had entered the race on the exchange with her. Fortunately, we had planned for an exchange that lap. As she wobbled back to the pit, I was on the bike sprinting back up to speed. Helping her onto a bike to warm down before her muscles seized up, Kevin changed the plan again. Amy had laid everything out on the track that day and raced a masterful race. But she was cooked. Kevin knew that Kirsten was equally potent in sprinting, so he told her that she would be the one to finish the race. Kirsten told me, later, that she was confident upon hearing this news: "No one was going to catch me. And if they did, I knew that I could beat them in the final sprint."

Meanwhile, I was in my last stint on the bike, and I was still in form somehow. Was it just the euphoria of the race? Actually, I think it was genetic, on account of my slow-twitch muscle fiber. One day when I was frustrated that I could not match her or Amy in sprinting, Kirsten had explained what she had learned in her exercise physiology class.

"People who are good at endurance sports have been proven to have a higher ratio of slow-twitch muscle fiber to fast-twitch muscle fiber," Kirsten said matter-of-factly. "That's you. I have a higher ratio of fast-twitch muscle fiber, probably, which is great for sprinting but not as good for lasting a long time. You can try to develop more fast-twitch or slow-twitch muscle fiber, but everyone's genes give them that higher or lower ratio of fast- to slow-twitch muscle." My genetic predisposition must have been linked to my dad. I had always been an endurance athlete—my talent, if I had one, was for going and going and going. Not too surprising for someone whose dad did ten-mile swim races and wanted to swim across the English Channel. Could be nature or could be nurture, but I was a long-haul athlete and not a sprinter.

Whether due to euphoria or slow-twitch muscle fiber, I was loving the catch-me-if-you-can racing. Of course, there's nothing not to like if you are the one to catch and in the lead by a decent margin. I felt somehow energized, riding my fastest laps of the entire race. *Don't even think about catching me*, I said, only in my mind, to the other teams. *Ain't gonna happen. Not me. Not today.* Then, *Love the pain*, trying to get myself to embrace going into the hurt zone. *Go, faster, come on, faster.* In my mind, I held the vision of myself increasing our advantage. I willed myself to perform at my best. If Lightning McQueen had been created back then, I would have been saying, "I am speed." But this was my own version.

I pushed through lactic acid and pain, motivated knowing this would be my last contribution to our team effort. My last chance to leave every ounce of my energy on the track was in those laps. Some laps in, the euphoria finally began to wear thin. My lungs started burning, my legs began aching, and I finally felt spent. Mind over matter, I powered through, but I started hoping, for the first time all day, to see Kevin's arms up when I came around the second corner and our pit came into sight. I no longer heard the crowd. I had tunnel vision. I was racing fast, but also just holding on.

Finally, Kevin gave me the sign: two laps to go. Things came back into focus. My hearing returned. Two laps, two-bike exchange. That meant Kirsten would come in to finish the race. I felt a surge in my energy level. It is funny how just knowing what you have left can make a difference. In that moment, knowledge gave me strength. I only had two laps to lay it down. Two laps all-out were what I planned to deliver. I knew that I could hold myself together that long. I dropped my head lower to minimize my drag. *Fast. Smooth*, I said to myself as I passed Kevin again. *Circles.* I focused on evening out my pedal strokes. One more lap. I had to leave Kirsten in good shape. I had no idea where the Thetas were or whether anyone else was advancing on us. I had not heard announcements over my own breathing, my own mind.

I came into the front stretch, passed the finish line, and headed toward our pit in my last lap of riding in the inaugural women's Little 500 race.

"As the Willkie Sprint rider comes across the start/finish line," said the booming voice of the announcer, "we now have just three laps. Three more laps for our leader." I heard the crowd let loose an enormous cheer. I put every last ounce of energy I had into that final turn, peeling outward toward our pit where Kirsten was waiting with her bike for the two-bike exchange. I jammed on the foot brake as she tagged my left forearm and sprinted off. Standing on the right pedal with all my weight, I skidded toward the default line by which I had to stop my bike, then jumped off in time to crouch low into my skid and lift my bike high in the air. It did not cross the line. We were done with exchanges!

I stood there a moment, so tired and out of breath that I was unable to do anything other than follow Kirsten's figure riding around the bottom of the oval. I caught Kirsten's expression as she rounded the corner. She looked strong. The expression on her face could be used as a visual representation by a dictionary defining the word *determination*. The Theta rider came by, and I visually measured the distance between her and Kirsten. Our lead was still sizable, more than a quarter lap. The Theta rider was leaning over her bike, and I could see that she too was giving everything she had. Although the Theta rider was strong on the bike and could not have been more motivated, Kirsten was every bit as fast. They seemed to be staying an equal distance apart from one another. I finally turned back to our pit. There is never certainty in a bike race, but the situation looked encouraging with under three laps to go. Unless something went wrong, it looked good.

"You OK?" Kevin had come over since I stood frozen with my bike. I nodded. "Come on, back to the pit." He put his arm around me and walked me over to a bike trainer. I did not get on it. I was too agitated. I wanted to stand and cheer for Kirsten. Amy was on her feet yelling across the track at Kirsten with all her might. Louise was milling around the pit nervously.

In the end, something did go wrong, and the Thetas did get a shot at catching us. Within a half lap of my exchange to Kirsten, time suddenly slowed down.

"Riders down! The yellow flag is out," came a booming announcement. "The yellow flag is out. Slow down, riders, and maintain your position relative to the race leader." *What?* The crowd hushed a moment while everyone sought out the site of the crash. It was hard to see from our pit, but it seemed that a few riders had gone down. At least one rider and bike was down on the track. Mechanics were running rampant, as they did when crashes occurred. Not knowing if their team riders were involved, they usually responded to news of a crash by running to the site with spare bikes in hand, just in case, because losing time was devastating for teams. I held my breath until I spotted Kirsten upright, not involved in the wreck. Phew!

Running the race under the yellow flag of caution allowed time for riders involved in the crash to get back up and going and time for any wreckage to be cleared. Riders were obligated to slow the pace. Race officials in every corner and straightaway gestured to all the riders like Kirsten who were not involved in the crash to slow down, just as Chappy Blackwell stood waving his yellow flag at the start/finish line.

And slow down Kirsten did. Boy, did she! We watched in dismay as she seemed to slow down to a snail's pace. In dismay because the teams chasing us did not slow down as much as Kirsten did. We watched Kirsten crawl along the front straightaway—and imagined our worst nightmare, being caught in the final laps.

"Oh no. She's going too slow," said Amy, watching them advance. "Come on, Kirsten!" She shouted it even though Kirsten was far away, across the track, and out of earshot. Wes started gesticulating wildly, as Kirsten ever so slowly entered turn one and would soon have our pit in view. We instantly joined in, all of us. It seemed as though riders near her had advanced on Kirsten on lap 98. Kirsten's pace was described by a newspaper article the next day as "super slo-mo." We could not believe our eyes. Riders were not allowed to advance on the leader under the yellow flag. It seemed to us that the chasing riders clearly had. No one said anything for a moment. We were all suddenly scared to death of what was to come. Would Kirsten get caught? In the final laps of the race?

"She can't do that," said Louise. "They're moving up under the yellow!" The yellow stayed out for more than an entire lap, but time stretched into eternity. Louise, Amy, Wes, and I were screaming like crazy, telling her to speed up. Even Kevin, who had kept his cool for the entire race, was agitated. As Kirsten passed, we went absolutely bonkers, motioning wildly for her to speed up, jumping up and down, and screaming our lungs out.

"The pack *must* slow down," boomed the announcer, seeming to have noticed the same thing that we had. "Team eight sets the pace." Relieved to hear the announcement, we watched to see whether the riders were still advancing. Maybe my mind was playing tricks on me, but it seemed that they were. *But you can't do that,* I said to myself. In the riders' defense, if they were actually advancing, it was probably only because Kirsten had slowed to an absolute crawl. Kirsten later told us that she had all the officials telling her to slow down. She felt that they were indicating that she needed to slow more than she had, and she was worried about being assessed a penalty if she did not slow enough. She knew that the creeping rule prevented other teams from advancing on her while under the yellow flag. So she slowed. And slowed. It was an unexpected turn of events after leading the race by a healthy margin for nearly sixty laps. Would the Theta rider or the others catch her?

I tried to recall the violation called "creeping" in the Little 500 race bible. It involved maintaining the track position and relative distance to the leader. But how flexible were they in applying that rule? There was no time to serve a penalty with only two laps left in the race, anyway. Would they even level a penalty at the Thetas, the beloved team who had fought to bring us the women's race in the first place, the reason we were all able to be here today? No way. I felt a real fear that things could go horribly wrong and an urgency to do something to stop it. I wished that I was on the bike myself, even though I knew Kirsten was wise, confident, and one of the strongest sprinters in the entire lot of riders. I had to trust that she would win—even if it was in a sprint after being caught by the other teams. I squeezed my gloved hands together in an involuntary prayer gesture. I faced away from the track for a moment of relief from the scene. I met eyes with Kristin, and we exchanged expressions loaded with the same one hundred emotions as we had earlier in the race. This time though, fear dominated the others.

"Oh my God," said Amy, dropping to the kneeling prayer position facing the pit board, unable to watch. "Kirsten better be ready to sprint."

"We are still under yellow" came another announcement, which I took as a confirmation that the riders were gaining on Kirsten. "We are under yellow. The pack must slow down."

"I just can't believe this," said Louise. We all stood helplessly hand-wringing and watching them coming through the far corner of the oval. It was downright painful to watch. The chasing riders seemed to have heard the message, but the gap between them and Kirsten seemed nonetheless smaller than it had been. Again, I wondered if my mind was playing tricks on me.

As Kirsten reached the front straightaway and the start/finish line, Chappy Blackwell delivered mercy and sweet relief in the form of the waving of the green flag. Kirsten still had a decent enough lead on the Theta rider, the next closest team. It might not have mattered anyway. Maybe she would have beaten her in a sprint. No one in our pit had wanted to find out. No one was happier than our team when the yellow lifted at the end of the ninety-eighth lap. Kirsten stood up and sprinted, taking off like a gunshot. The collective sigh of our team and our entire section of fans was audible. I took a deep breath, feeling as if I had surfaced after being underwater, holding my breath, during the drama of the last lap and a half.

"And you will see Chappy Blackwell now with the flag, ladies and gentlemen," boomed the announcer. "We are live... All teams can return to racing." And then again, "We are back racing." Kirsten emptied every last ounce of her energy into an amazing lap. We cheered like mad when she passed on that ninety-ninth lap. In the one-third of a lap since the green flag had returned, Kirsten had taken off like a rocket and regained any ground lost between her and the others in spades. Our fans thundered in support. Kirsten was on a terrific pace. The Theta rider came through the corner at a quarter lap behind, and I wanted to cheer for her too. She was one of the founding mothers of this race. She merited all the applause of the entire crowd.

"Our leader, Willkie Sprint, is getting the white flag. One lap to go," said the announcer as the spectators went wild, all of them throughout the stadium, cheering their teams to a strong finish and cheering for us all. "The white flag is out." Chappy Blackwell waved the flag with flair. He, like the flag-bearer of the Indianapolis car race, took the job of flag waving to the level of sport, moving his whole body back and forth as he continued waving the flag for all the riders who passed to signal the final lap. An announcement had been made reminding everyone that the first ten teams could finish their one hundred laps even if they had been lapped. All others were to finish on the same lap as the leader. All eyes were focused on turn two. Kirsten rounded the turn for the final time, in the one-hundredth lap, at the same breakneck pace as the previous lap. She was on fire.

Wes shot his hands high in the air, already claiming victory. Kevin was crouching to Kirsten's level and his hands still pedaling, but he stood and clapped as she headed past and down the straightaway. Each of our faces turned from nervous concentration and concern to incredulous joy when we saw the one-third lap advantage. Kirsten finished the race absolutely flying.

As she went across the finish line, Chappy Blackwell dramatically waved the checkered flag. "Willkie Sprint crosses the line," said the announcer, "the winners of the first women's Little 500 race in one hour, ten minutes, and fifty-two seconds!"

Exhausted from her effort, Kirsten remembered a discussion from the night before about doing an extra lap just in case there had been a miscount. To make sure that the victory was secure—after our one hundred laps of all-out effort—Kirsten completed another lap out in front. Only then, once she knew that we had the secure and legitimate win, did she celebrate by lifting a single arm, clenching her left fist and raising it in the air in victory. We had done it!

Meanwhile, we had exploded in celebration in the pit. There was a contagious case of near ecstasy. I turned to Kristin and reached over the pit boards, and we rocked back and forth in a big hug.

My sister Ann, visibly ecstatic about the win, had pushed up front to do the same. Amy, Louise, Kevin, Wes, and I jumped up and down, screamed, hugged, shrieked, and basked in the limelight and the cheering of the crowd. Our decisive victory made it worth all the hours it had taken to get there. Kirsten arrived on the bike, and we surrounded her. We exalted together as if we had won the lottery. Because we felt as if we had. We had prepared ourselves to win the race physically but not psychologically. Nothing could have prepared us for the magical feeling of winning the inaugural Little 500 race in front of a live crowd of fifteen thousand rowdy students and fans.

"I can't believe it. This is crazy!" shouted Amy. It was. For us, it would have been glorious enough to have won the race in a stadium empty of fans or in a triumphant final sprint from the peloton at the finish. We would have gone crazy. To have won the coveted Little 500 race in such a decidedly strong fashion, out in front and maintaining a gap for over seventy-five laps, was such an important affirmation of all our hard work. To have done so in front of a stadium packed with fans and reporters sweetened the victory so much more. The hundred emotions that had been brewing inside of us all race long, really all year long, spilled out.

"Did you know there'd be all these reporters?" asked Louise. Our joy was being captured by scores of photographers who were part of the large press corps that had gathered on the infield. Around forty journalists stood on the infield directly across from our pit. All of them were documenting the historical first for women at Indiana University. They had come from around the country, including a reporter from the *New York Times*. The press had gravitated toward our pit, growing in number throughout the race as it seemed increasingly likely that our team would hold on to the lead. Their respective newspapers would splash photos of us all over the city, state, and even nation the next day.

After dumping water over Kevin's head and having it dumped over my own, I ran over to give hugs to the Theta riders and any other rider I saw. The Thetas' emotions were on the surface. We congratulated one another. I told them that they had set a spectacular event in motion.

"I can't believe that we were able to beat you guys. You are our heroes. Everyone's heroes," I said. I meant it. I almost felt bad that they had not won. I almost felt bad that we had beaten them. Almost.

I also knew though that our victory was hard-earned. I walked back to our pit and searched for my dad and Rob in the crowd. Towering over the others was Dad. He smiled widely and gave me a double thumbs-up. Rob was there smiling too. I hurried over to hug them. After some celebrating with our team's race-day fans, we were summoned to the infield to chat with reporters and make our way toward the awards ceremony.

"Kerry, I peed my pants," said Louise in a hushed tone as we headed toward the infield, "jumping up and down, in those final laps." I burst out laughing. "Not a ton," she said, "but still. Pretty embarrassing."

"No way," I said, checking her out visually. "Well, you can't tell at all, if that helps. I've always said that the chamois in cycling shorts is like wearing a diaper."

We giggled and recounted to reporters interviewing us everything about our year of training and how it felt to win, except of course that detail. With Malcolm Moran, the journalist sent by the *New York Times*, I shared our restrictive diet. I sort of regretted that when my quote, "No drinking. No sugar" became a subheading within the *NYT* article. Seeing it in print almost made me wish that I hadn't waxed poetic. But in those moments of post-race joy, my teammates and I were bubbling with words, excitement over our win, and nostalgia about how we got there.

We moved on to the presentation of the awards on the podium. With great enthusiasm, *the* Bill Armstrong for whom the Little 500 track and soccer stadium had been named presented us with a large golden trophy with a cyclist riding atop the cup. We relished the moment, lifting our race bicycle and trophies high in the air. There was a second trophy that we were only allowed to handle that day. It was the Little 500 race's famous Borg-Warner trophy. On display throughout the year at the IU Memorial Union, it was a replica of the revered Indianapolis 500 trophy that immortalized the name and face of each year's Indy 500 race winner. We took turns admiring and holding the sacred trophy.

The hoopla of racing, cheers, interviewing, awards, and celebration at the Bill Armstrong Stadium finally died down a good hour or two after the race. The sun was setting on our spectacular day. I noticed Kevin staring toward the sunset. His pink shirt had come partially untucked. Was he thinking of his mom? Words would not do. I stepped toward him and gave him a strong hug.

Together as a team, we brought our trophy back to put in our dorm's glass case. We found out that Steve Tesich had called the dormitory looking for us. Tesich was the screenwriter who had won an Oscar for Best Screenplay for the film *Breaking Away*. It turned out that the story was based in part on Tesich's own experience riding as a member of the Phi Kappa Psi fraternity's bicycle team, which had won the Little 500 race in the 1960s. Tesich was living out in New York, and he had somehow heard about the first women's race taking place that afternoon. Interested in talking with us, Tesich had confirmed a specific time later that evening in which he would call again. We were ready for showers, so we gave our individual room phone numbers. An hour later, he took the time to call each of us individually.

"Congratulations on winning the race! I bet that was a lot of fun," said the cheery voice on the other end. "I experienced those same emotions many years ago myself. It's wonderful that you women can now experience the Little 500. I guess it's about time." From his manner of speaking, I found Steve Tesich to be kind and sincere.

"Thanks," I said. "Yeah, it was really incredible. I can't stop smiling!" Tesich told me that the glow of winning would last. (I eventually found out that he was right—when I was still wearing my perma-grin days later.)

"Tell me," Steve Tesich said, "who—which actress—would be best to play you, if there is a film made about the women's race? Some kind of sequel to *Breaking Away*."

"To play me?" I said. The question surprised me.

"Yes, in the film version," he said. "Who would be the right choice? Is there a Hollywood actor that would be perfect for the role?"

"Hmm," I said, "I'm not really sure. People always tell me that I look a lot like the character Jo on the TV sitcom *Facts of Life*. But I am not sure if that's just because I am a bit of a tomboy like her." I later learned that he had asked the same question of the others. Maybe he would write the film someday.

I told Steve Tesich that I really loved *Breaking Away*, that we had watched it together before the race, and that it gave us inspiration. How often I would watch the film again over the years following my conversation with its screenwriter! And not because I had met Tesich over the phone. *Breaking Away* had cult movie status in Bloomington. It was sometimes shown as the midnight movie at the Memorial Union's movie theater. You never get the chance to meet the person who wrote a movie you loved. I told him how we had vowed to go find the limestone quarries.

There was something else too: I felt an emotional tie to Tesich that I would experience throughout the subsequent years with others who had taken part in the Little 500 race. It was a sense of commonality. And a shared love for the Little 500 experience. It was something that I would come across again and again, a common tie with all those who had taken part in the wondrous central event of the World's Greatest College Weekend, for which we might all justly thank Howdy Wilcox and Herman B Wells. The female contingent might add Amelia and her feminist friends, Phyllis Klotman, and all the female students who fought over the years for our right to be there, to have the same special experience previously available only to the men.

CHAPTER

"HON, YOU DIDN'T TELL ME what a big deal this race was," said my dad the following morning. "I had no idea. I mean, fifteen thousand people watching, that's a *big deal*." We were eating omelets and French toast at another favorite for Rob and me: the Runcible Spoon, Bloomington's hip and eclectic coffee shop that roasted their own beans in-house. Long before Starbucks expanded beyond Seattle, the Runcible Spoon fully captured the ambience of a European café. Inspired by the smell of roasting coffee filling the cozy restaurant, I ordered a cappuccino, selecting the Italian morning classic from a full page of coffee drink offerings.

We had about seven newspapers splayed out on the table before us. As they were leaving their hotel down in Lawrence County that morning, before their half-hour drive up to Bloomington, Dad and Ann had caught a picture of my teammates and me on the front page of a local newspaper. They stopped at a gas station to purchase their own copy and saw that we graced the front page of a number of the papers on display. They bought them all. Fortunately, it distracted my dad from his irritation about how far away the hotel was. When I met Dad in the dorm parking lot with Rob to head out for brunch together, he told me first about the articles and second about how far away their hotel was. ("We're really *out* there! Was that all you could find?")

I considered Dad's comment about the race for a minute.

"How could I tell you what to expect when *I* didn't even know?" I said.

"I'm pretty sure that even IUSF did not expect that kind of a turnout, even if they hoped for it," said Rob, looking up from an article he was reading. Then, quoting an Indianapolis newspaper, he said, "Get this: the Theta's coach says he was simply 'outcoached.' That's big, coming from him."

I explained to my dad and sister that the Theta's coach was very experienced from numerous years of coaching men's teams. Kevin was going to love that quote.

We had a good laugh at the half-page photo that captured a close-up of Kirsten dumping the water cooler on Kevin but also caught my sister Ann in the background, looking cool with her shades and big smile. Dad was most impressed by the article accompanied by a sizable photo of Amy, Louise, and me in the *New York Times*.

"The *New York Times*, that's big, kid! You might never get a mention there for the rest of your life," said Dad. I felt like he might be underestimating me but did not say anything since I realized that it was quite possibly me underestimating the difficulty of landing in the *New York Times*.

Later we headed off to see the men's Little 500 race, where I would reap some unexpected benefits of our victory. It was a full hour before the race start time, but the Bill Armstrong Stadium was already packed. My teammates and I had an appointment with Tom Ehrlich, the president of the university. Seriously. As Little 500 champions from the women's race, we were invited to meet Ehrlich and his wife, Ellen, on the infield of the track prior to the men's event. They were enthusiastic, and Ellen Ehrlich, decked out in IU memorabilia, was particularly excited about the women's race.

As we were chatting with President Ehrlich, our attention was directed to the sky above. A brightly colored parachute and skydiver approached, delivering a giant billowing American flag. I then realized the reason why a giant circular IUSF symbol had appeared a few days earlier in the very center of the infield. It was the landing target for the skydiver.

Looking up, we shielded our eyes from the sunshine and cheered loudly as we witnessed a perfect landing.

"You gotta be kidding me," said Amy, squinting upward.

"This is over the top," Louise said. "A skydiver?"

"Hey, how come we didn't get a skydiver for our race?" asked Kirsten.

"Ohhh-eee, Coach Yeagley and his staff would be kicking booty and takin' names if they saw all this action on their precious soccer field," I said, thinking about how many times I had heard them issue grumpy (but understandable) requests to stay off the infield. Today it was full of journalists, mechanics, and now, a skydiver coming in to land right in the middle of the field.

Along with the Ehrlichs, we were asked to ride in the shiny red Sunbird convertibles during the parade laps for the men's race. We sat protruding from one of the five shiny convertibles, following the Ehrlichs' car and the others who shared the honor of riding in the convertibles on the parade lap. One Sunbird held the Little 500 King and Queen (no kidding), who sat with MTV hosts Adam Sandler and Downtown Julie Brown. The MTV cameraman knelt in the front seat filming, while VJ Adam Sandler held a sign off-camera reading, "Go NUTS for MTV!" You can only imagine the response of a fully packed stadium of college kids at the crown jewel event of the World's Greatest College Weekend.

Since we had won, my team and I were given passes to watch the men's Little 500 bike race from the two-level press box up in the old north-side stands. I brought Rob with me. We entered and realized immediately that this was the VIP seating, and the very important persons of most interest to us were IU's best ever football star, Anthony Thompson, and John Mellencamp. Thompson was a star running back and had been a candidate for the Heisman that year. Mellencamp was Bloomington royalty but was also a deserving VIP on account of giving the most attended Little 500 concert ever two years earlier. Concerts had long been a staple of Little 500 weekend. Mellencamp had apparently risen to the occasion of a large hometown crowd and given a spectacular performance, rumored to have been one of his best ever, to a packed IU Memorial (football) Stadium. Tickets sold out nearly instantaneously, and in addition to the forty-three thousand concert-goers in the stadium, an estimated ten thousand additional fans enjoyed the show from the surrounding parking lot area.

Mellencamp's rock-star aura of coolness made him somehow both glittering and familiar. I suppose that was because we had seen a lot of Mellencamp's face in that era of MTV videos, not to mention on his album covers and posters. Rob took a stab at conversation.

"Hey, how's it goin'?" he said, in a tone trying so hard to imbue coolness that we laughed about it later.

Mellencamp was cordial but pretty brief with us. We got the message and wandered off to watch the race. There was one thing that struck me. Maybe it is because I am tall, but I think it's also that we tend to expect stars to be truly bigger than life itself. Or at least bigger than we are. The reality was that in person Mellencamp was an inch or two shorter than me. Of course, it did not matter at all, but I was surprised. Engaging in small talk face to face with a rock star was pretty awesome. When we left the press box later, I found him just outside, smoking a cigarette. He smiled and said, "Can't last too long without one of these." I responded that he did well to get a break from the stuffiness inside and headed off to watch the race.

The men's Little 500 race seemed a long and drawn-out version of our race the day before. There were double the number of spectators—the stands and bleachers were all packed, and the newspaper the next day reported twenty-eight thousand fans in attendance! Entire fraternities were seated together behind their teams cheering loudly and drunkenly under the beating sun. By the end of the race, there had been numerous attempts to break away by various teams, but nine teams were still together going into the final lap. Jay Polsgrove, a rider for the Cutters, the independent team adopting the team name of *Breaking Away*'s main characters, reeled in and then broke decisively from the others in the last half lap. He won the race with a brilliant sprint.

As I watched the fans erupt with cheers, I reflected on my own experience but also on what the popularity of the race and all those people watching meant for IU. Each had purchased a ticket, which was valid for both the men's and women's races. The incoming cash from ticket sales provided scholarships. Howdy Wilcox Jr. had come up with a winning recipe, from what I could see. Thousands of alumni reminisced, thousands of students celebrated, and hundreds of riders created great memories during Little 500. Just by participating, each of us had enriched our freshman experience immeasurably. The race provided scholarships for working students with a minimum GPA. Kirsten was working in a lab on campus. I was working in the dorm cafeteria. We knew how much difference a little money could make to a working student.

"You know, you're lucky you were born when you were," Dad said later. "Your timing here was perfect, after Title IX has really gone into effect." I had heard of Title IX but was not really sure what it was. But my dad is an encyclopedia—and was also a career university dean with a love for all, but particularly college, sports. For a while, he even served on the Athletic Board at University of Wisconsin.

"See, in the 1970s," he said, "they passed this law saying no one could be excluded from any educational program or activity, like sports, at any institution receiving federal funding. Well, that includes all big universities. Took 'em a while to figure out how to apply the law, because it was buried in some civil rights legislation. Eventually Title IX, which was actually just one sentence, was interpreted to mean that there had to be the same number of participants in sports for both genders and the same number of scholarships given to men and women." Dad displayed a look of surprise, reflecting how the university sporting programs must have felt at the time. "The same numbers! After all those years of not even having women's teams.

"I mean, hey, Title IX was a really big deal," he said. "Still is. It's created all sorts of problems for universities—they've had to balance out the number of spots in sports like wrestling and football, where there were no women's teams, by adding programs for women. Same for scholarships. The UW crew team, for example, has all sorts of scholarships for women but not a single one for the guys' team. Football takes 'em all. Can you imagine how that's changed things?"

All the specifics of Title IX were news to me, although I had benefited enormously from the changing winds, and attitudes, toward equality of opportunity for women, brought by the law. It was a correction of the historic gendered preference for men's sports. I thought of my friend Margaret, swimming on a full scholarship at UW. She was lucky that she had not been born ten years earlier and arrived in college before Title IX was being enforced. Since the Little 500 was just an intramural collegiate activity, not an NCAA sport, it was not strictly beholden to the same standard of Title IX. It took countless courageous riders and Phyllis Klotman to push the agenda of Title

IX into the Little 500 arena. So again, I say my thank-yous to all of them, from Amelia on forward.

Of course, they are not just women, those to whom I owe thanks. The Title IX legislation had been proposed by Indiana's native son Senator Birch Bayh, who had written, introduced, and sponsored the bill. His son Evan Bayh happened to be gearing up a campaign for governor during my freshman year, and the elder Bayh came to Bloomington in support of the effort. I met him that year at a small Honors Division event at the Haskett House. He spoke to a group of us about the equality of rights for all genders and races. If I had known then about his efforts and that he was the founding father of the Title IX legislation, I would have thanked Birch Bayh heartily in person that day.

"Keep your nose to the grindstone," said Dad as I gave giant parting hugs to him and Ann before they drove off on the long journey back to Wisconsin. "Mom and I are so proud of you." With his mention of schoolwork, I felt the weight of all the end-of-semester academic work settle on my shoulders. Rob and I had decided that we needed to buckle down and study like mad. Final exams were coming up, and we both wanted to finish strong. Loaded down with books, we headed off to study, hand in hand.

"Hey," I asked Rob later as we admired a flowering dogwood tree on campus, "why does your friend Jim call you Bob?" I had noticed that Jim, Rob's visiting high school friend, referred to him as "Bob."

"Well yeah, so that's basically what everyone has always called me," Rob (Bob?) said. I was confused. "I'm named after my uncle Bob, which is cool and all. I just thought that coming to college, it would be a good time to start going by Robert instead of Bob. You know, kind of drop the kid version and get more serious." *What?* This was news to me. Why hadn't he told me his real name?

"Well," he continued, "it didn't really work out because right away after like a week, everyone just shortened it to Rob."

"Which is, I guess, the same as Bob, kind of?" I chuckled, trying to make sense of this news. "It's definitely not Robert. Wow, I can't believe you never told me! It's actually pretty funny."

"I know," he said, "it is! I just didn't really know what to do." He looked a little embarrassed about the whole thing. "Should I just stick with Rob? I still haven't gotten used to it."

"I don't know. My family calls me KK or Kake or a bunch of other nick-names. I like them better than Kerry because the people who know me best use them," I offered. I understood, sort of. But not really.

"I have no idea," I continued. "Guess the whole Robert thing backfired. These are first-world problems. Just choose the one you like best, I guess. But nice try, on invoking the coolness of Robert Kennedy. Yours truly's got a new name for you. I'm going to call you Rob-Bob." He laughed. I think he felt relieved at having outed his name-identity crisis. It was our favorite joke for a while.

The next day, when I walked into my Imagining Nature class, my class-mates broke out in spontaneous applause. Professor Sanders joined in. I felt my face flush with color. It was three days post-race, and I was still wearing a smile wherever I went. I had been surprised at how many people knew that we had won and congratulated me, in our dorm and around campus. I had heard that the winners of the men's Little 500 had rock-star status on campus. The heightened attention and media coverage of the inaugural women's race gave us a similar effect.

Later in our class discussion of *Arctic Dreams* by Barry Lopez, Scott Sand-ers referred to Lopez's description of observing the migration of snow geese.

"I loved that part," I said. Lopez had written that the birds migrating over-head calmed him and reminded him of life's "oldest mysteries: the nature and extent of space, the fall of light from the heavens, the pooling of time in the present, as if it were water."

"Did it remind you of anything that you've experienced?" Professor Sand-ers asked me.

"Back when I read it," I said, "I thought of my family's cabin at Sunday Lake with its loons and eagles." I paused, expecting that for most, the passage had likely evoked the same, moments of calm that came from being in nature.

"OK," said Professor Sanders, nodding and understanding there was more, "and now?"

"Well, now," I said, "I was just thinking that those words—the light falling from the heavens, and 'the pooling of time in the present'—kind of remind me of how it felt to win the Little 500." My face reddened again, embarrassed to have brought up winning the race. But those words really did neatly define the feeling of glory that day.

There was another evening of celebrating that following week at the Little 500 Victory Banquet. All men's and women's teams were present in the grand Alumni Hall at the Memorial Union. It was fun to see everyone dressed up for the event, finally ditching Lycra for a dinner engagement in semi-formal dress. Everyone was so clean and beautified.

"You bruisers clean up pretty nicely," said our friend Sue from the Cycle-delics team as she entered with us. It was five days since our victory at the race, and it was nice to see everyone. My life had taken on a new rhythm—no track practice and a lot more studying to make sure that I exited from the semester with a respectable report card.

As we entered the Alumni Hall, each team was asked to vote on the recipients of the All-Star Rider and Rookie of the Year Awards. The criteria for All-Star Rider included top results in the Little 500 race and Series, leadership qualities, and congeniality. The Rookie Award—designed for those riding in the race for the first time, which in this inaugural year included the entire field of women's riders—was based on riding skill, number of laps ridden in the race, and performance in Quals and the Series events. Both awards were determined by peer vote. We discussed fervently which of our friends from other teams were most deserving of the honors and entered our votes.

There was also the Hall of Fame rider award. Names suggested by a special standing committee had to be ratified by at least one-half of the teams, or alternatively, others not listed could be elected to the Hall of Fame by a two-thirds write-in majority. My team instantly agreed to nominate two Theta riders for the Hall of Fame.

The men's teams were rowdy even throughout the meal, but they really lit up and cheered energetically for every award given. Winning the first Little 500 race itself had been more than enough for me. So I was honored and surprised when my name was read as one of four to receive the Rookie of the Year Award. No sooner had I returned to my seat than they announced my name as one of the winners of the eight All-Star Rider Awards. Kirsten was also named a recipient, and we headed to the podium together, along with some favorite companions from other teams: Jill, Mia, Sue, Suzi, and two Theta riders. I was emotional and humbled by receiving both awards, especially because of the peer voting. Our team's table was eventually piled high with trophies and awards, but those two plaques for rider honors that I did not even know existed before that evening held as much meaning as anything else shining on our table. I was touched.

For winning the race, that night we were awarded winners' rings, the Little 500 version of those given for the Indy 500 win. Kevin received his own coach's ring. The idea of championship rings was familiar to me from the NBA and the Super Bowl, but receiving one for winning the race was another surprise of the evening. We put them on and posed for photos holding our hands out, just as a freshly engaged woman might. The round of applause from our fellow athletes was as rewarding as the cheering stadium had been. The students in Alumni Hall that evening knew all about the balancing act of training for Little 500 while taking a full load of classes. I applauded them as well. They had done the same, and crossing the finish line first did not make our efforts any different.

Most poignant in the end, of course, was my tribe, the team members seated around our table. The bonds with Kristin, Amy, Louise, Kirsten, and Kevin had shaped and enriched my life that year. Our scrappy ragtag team had united to pull off an all-freshman win, upsetting the expectations that the Theta team would get the first trophy, which we had all believed was rightfully theirs. In doing so, we had developed solid friendships with one another that meant more than the victory ever could.

Studying with Rob the next day, I was finishing up writing the persuasive speech I had to give in my public speaking class. I had decided on the topic "Why you should ride in the Little 500." Rob was a big fan of the *Late Night with Dave Letterman* show, and we had started watching it regularly. Letterman's humorous Top Ten Lists were my favorite part, I guess because of their ridiculousness. Preparing my speech, I decided the top-ten format would work out well. I would avoid humor and give serious reasons, but I thought the format could maybe make it fun and convincing.

"OK, here's what I was thinking," I said to Rob during our study break. "I'm working on my speech. I decided to go Letterman-style. I'm going to give you the practice run of the top ten reasons why you should ride in the Little 500 race. I think the prof. will go for this, but honestly, I am not sure. So here goes.

"Number ten: riding in Little 500 introduces you to the great sport of cycling. Getting regular exercise is good for you, and cycling is a lifetime sport. That means you can stick with it for your entire life. It's non-jarring, so it is easy on your joints, and you can go at your own pace. You couldn't find a better activity to start now as a college student. Plus, you'll understand a lot more about the Tour de France and the Olympic cycling races when you watch them." That weekend, my dad had told me how cycling was something that could carry me through my whole life, like swimming had for him, and he'd explained the concept of a lifetime sport.

"Number nine: you'll get in amazing shape, maybe the best shape of your life. The teams that take this race seriously train most of the academic school year, but even the others have to meet mandatory minimum requirements including a certain number of hours training on the track and participation in some other Little 500 Series events. Looking good and being fit helps you land a date for Friday nights too." Here Rob nodded and snickered. I went on.

"Number eight: you will have an excuse to get off campus. . . . I'm not sure," I said, pausing and looking up from my speech notes to Rob, "whether I should say that, or one of these: you'll get to know all the beautiful countryside around Bloomington, or you'll discover a bunch of lakes all within riding distance—and they're all beautiful! But, anyway, then I'll tell them all about how pretty all the little roads into the country are. How spectacular the hills and views are around here. Or about Lakes Lemon, Griffy, and Monroe. Not sure I'll mention Pirate. I could mention how we once stopped during a ride at Lake Lemon and learned there was an IU sailing facility there." Rob and I had decided that the following semester we would sign up for a sailing course there for university credit. Rob nodded and waved his hand in a circle, which meant to keep going and he'd give me his opinion later.

"Number seven: You get to ride around a track, and you'll learn how to do a bike exchange." I looked up at Rob. I had not yet drafted this part. "Here, basically, I am going to tell them how fun the track is. Then I'll explain how you do an exchange and tell them how cool it feels to master them. How it's just like when you master skiing, shoot free throws, or anything else.

"Number six: you'll get better grades. Well, there's no actual proof for this, except my own example. I did better this semester because I had to organize myself way more. So even though I was busier—training a lot and doing the Series events on the weekends—I got better grades because I had to be organized and focused." I paused, looked at Rob, and conceded: "That's not my favorite one, but it's true, so I felt like it could be convincing.

"Number five. The fifth best reason to take part in the Little 500 bike race is you might just win. Who knows? If you do win, you will experience intense and profound joy and a validation of all the time you spent training. Thousands of people will cheer you on either way, but if you win, they'll go nuts when you do. You'll get all sorts of attention from the media and then around campus too. You'll be smiling for days.

"Number four: racing in Little 500 will create memories that shape your college career and last a lifetime. Like spending your Sunday mornings going on training rides together with your team. Or weekday afternoons hanging out at the track practicing. Like all the moments spent waiting and watching with other teams at Qualifications or the other Little 500 Series races. Like laughing together when dogs chase you on rides and crying when you crash or botch an important exchange. It's all that camaraderie that makes it such a great experience. You'll be the ones who can really call it the World's Greatest College Weekend.

"Number three: the proceeds from the Little 500 race provide scholarships for working students. This could qualify for the number one reason, because giving back is so important in life. The success of the race depends on having student athletes dedicated to competing for fun and glory. The more we support the race by having full fields of riders in both races and by encouraging people to go watch it, the more the number of scholarships offered each year can grow. It's not about the race; it's about helping your fellow students—those who are already balancing studying with working." Affirming head nodding from Rob.

"Number two. The second-best reason to ride in the Little 500 race: your mom couldn't. It's true. Our mothers' generation did not have the same opportunities. There were not many sports available in general for women before they started enforcing Title IX in the early 1980s. That's the law that changed things. Title IX established that all sporting and educational activities had to be offered equally to both sexes at institutions that get federal funding. Your mom didn't have your options, and neither, probably, did your older sister. *This year* was the first year that women could race in the Little 500. So, no matter what your sex, ride Little 500, because your mom couldn't." Rob gave me a nod and thumbs-up. He liked that one. I was sure he'd like the next one too.

"Number one: your teammates and riders from other teams will become some of your closest friends. You spend so much time together training and bonding on long bike rides, you really get to know your teammates. Then at the track, you spend a lot of time getting to know the other teams too. You have so much fun together. It's really bonding. Then, if you are lucky enough to have co-ed teams like I did at my dorm—well, of course, it could happen even if it's a same-sex team—you might just meet someone really cool, really special on your team, and fall in love. Like I did." Rob smiled but still held back any comment until I finished.

"So there you have it, folks! The top ten reasons to go out and find yourself a Little 500 team when you get back to Bloomington next fall. It will enhance your college experience for the better!"

Rob stood up, clapped, and cheered. We hugged. He was my number one fan, and I was his. My heart was full. Winning Little 500 had only been the *second* best thing that had happened to me that year.

"Brava!" he said, getting the feminine tense right in Italian. "I give you an A." Of course he was bound to like it, biased as he was. It was the story of my freshman year, much of which we had lived through together.

It was the story that, thirty-plus years later, the film producer wanted to put on the big screen. There was no doubt that it had been a great nine months in my life. A spectacular start to college. I had no idea if it would make a good story on the big screen. I only knew that my experience that year gave me my first love, a set of rich friendships, an introduction to the wonderful sport of bicycling, an understanding of my place in the world as both a woman and a product of my family life, and an implausible victory in the Little 500 race, the amazing and historically significant event that I had barely heard of a year earlier.

Each member of my team and each participant in the women's Little 500 race has their own story of that year. Mine is inextricably linked to who I was when I moved into my eleventh-floor room at Willkie North dormitory in August 1987. The team, teammates, and training so dominated my year that my 1988 inaugural Little 500 story is that of my freshman year of college. The story of leaving home, landing in Bloomington, starting anew, falling in love, figuring out where I stood, and emerging as an adult. Mine is a story of coming of age.

14

CHAPTER

THE LITTLE 500 RACE shaped my collegiate experience. I competed in the race for all four years. When we came back to IU in the fall of 1988 following our victory, I moved off-campus to the house with Karen, Tara, and others. Louise did not race again and ended up finishing her degree in Kentucky. Kristin was in her senior year and chose to focus her time on other things that year. Amy, Kirsten, and I would race together as Team Sprint, having lost our affiliation to Willkie. Kevin coached us once again.

In 1989, missing Kristin and Louise for the second edition of the race, we were joined by two strong riders, Mia and Jen, from another team that had broken up. We became what the Thetas had been the previous year, the team to beat. In an unfortunate last-minute turn, our team was assessed a penalty, announced just the evening before the race. Unbeknownst to us, our mechanic had put an illegal part on our race bike. Kevin was furious. We all were. The penalty would cost us our best shot at winning the second edition of the race. We served it early but doing so put us behind the team who ended up winning the race, Beyond Control. We chased them the entire race, just as other teams had chased us the previous year, and finished in a very disappointing second place.

In 1990, the third year of the women's race, we raced again as Team Sprint and came in hungry to redeem ourselves. Since Kevin had graduated, Kirsten, who was busy working and unable to make the time commitment to training, became our coach. Amy, Mia, and I were joined by a fourth rider, Heidi. The overall level of preparedness and fitness increased steeply in the first few years, and the field became deeper with more teams capable of winning. We battled much of the race with several strong teams but were able to gain an advantage around lap 70. We were able to hold on to our lead. Amy crossed the finish line with a healthy gap. We claimed our second victory. It was as sweet as the first, although Kirsten, Amy, and I recognized that there was only *one inaugural* race, and our second win was not as historical.

In 1991, as a senior, I was the only member of our original Willkie Sprint team left at IU. Kirsten and Amy had both managed to graduate early. I had been a member of the Riders' Council organizing the race throughout college. I had grown to love the event and the opportunity it offered women even more. However, there had been a dip in participation, and very few women's teams were signed up. That year, I committed myself to riding with new riders who might not otherwise race in Little 500. I recruited a friend from the English honor's program and two others who had shown interest at a call-out meeting. My English department friend dropped out, and we ended up riding with just three on race day. In my final race, our three-rider Team Sprint finished in fifth place.

My preference for adventure continued for years. As did my love of Rob-Bob. (Not in that order.) We adventured happily together for fifteen years. After going to law school, spending a winter in a log cabin in Grand Teton National Park, and doing Peace Corps in Papua New Guinea, we landed back in Madison, where I started riding on a local women's cycling team.

I had some good fortune on the bike and went on to race professionally. Looking to train at altitude, I talked Bob into moving to Boulder, Colorado. Then, for my last two seasons of racing, I managed to jump to the top level. We moved to Italy, and I raced for an Italian team. We lived in team housing on Lake Iseo, charming but less touristy than the more famous northern lakes, Como and Garda.

At that time, many of the best cyclists in the international women's peloton lived and trained in Italy, particularly down in Tuscany. The weather was milder, and Italians gave recognition and financial sponsorship (although minimal) to women's cycling teams. More important, every weekend the best in the world lined up together. Racing on an Italian team was like riding the World Championships every weekend. I was in heaven. It was perfect preparation for the World Cup races, but for me, it was more. Standing on the start line, I might chat with Germans, Aussies, Spaniards, Dutchies, Kiwis, or Brits. Many became close friends, as did my Italian, Swiss, Russian, and American teammates.

While I loved racing at that level, I was definitely not winning races. Far from it. I took on the role of *domestique*, providing support for our team leaders. My job was often to attack over and over early in the race or to cover the early attacks by others. Other times, I might deliver water, food, or clothing, dropping back to the team vehicle and then up to the team leaders, thus allowing them to save their energy for winning the race. Many of my teammates and friends from the international peloton rode and medaled in the Sydney and Athens Olympic Games.

I had parlayed my humble beginnings in the Little 500 race into participating in the women's Tour de France—in my era named the Grande Boucle Féminine Internationale and consisting of a two-week stage race around the beautiful French countryside—and the Tour of Italy, also a two-week stage race, called the Giro d'Italia Donne. A bonus to competing at the highest level was racing, eating, and soaking in the culture on our way through the amazing country of Italy and around the world. We were thrilled to be living in Italy, and racing in the elite peloton was the realization of a dream for me. I was even able to finally use the language skills that I had acquired taking Italian back at IU. Unfortunately, I had a devastating fall, in which I broke my femur, in the 2001 Giro d'Italia Donne. I decided to retire from professional racing, and we returned to Boulder, where Rob-Bob and I eventually headed our separate ways.

Since then, I have repeated the move to Italy twice. My sons, Gino and Giorgio, were born in Italy during a stint living in the Alpine paradise of their father's hometown, Bormio—an epically beautiful mountain town in the shadow of the mythical Stelvio and Gavia passes, which I managed to ride as much as pregnancy and motherhood allowed (far less than I might have liked).

In our most recent move, already ten years ago now, my family and I returned to Italy, this time to Trento in the spectacular Dolomite mountains. Here I regularly ride my bicycle all over the Italian terrain that I fell in love with back in my racing years.

Italy has cycling teams for kids, adorable with their crooked helmets and little legs so skinny that their Lycra cycling shorts are baggy. They start as young as five years old, riding around on the smallest road bikes you have ever seen. Hoping to inspire in them the same appreciation that I have for riding a bicycle, I stuck both my sons on a local cycling team in Trento, Club Ciclistico Gardolo. I volunteered to help out with team practice sessions, hoping to watch my kids and the others develop the passion for cycling that I had.

Indeed, Gino and Giorgi gained an appreciation for both a spirited ride enjoying the company of their teammates and the sport of cycling in general. Every May, we watch the Giro d'Italia stage in which the pro peloton passes closest to our city, waiting faithfully on the roadside for the colorful cyclists to arrive. When they do, the boys shout out "*borraccia!*" (water bottle) in the hope that the pros will toss a team water bottle their way. Cycling is intense and hard to balance with other sports, and ultimately both boys have opted out, but I am happy they each gave cycling a whirl. As they approach college age, I occasionally mention IU and the Little 500 as a potential option of interest. My kids, of course, have their own ideas, dreams, and aspirations, and they will choose their own paths. I wish only to support them in the same way my parents supported me.

During the past fifteen years, I have channeled my passion for cycling another way. When I lived in Boulder, Colorado, I had the good fortune of becoming friends with Andy Hampsten and eventually his wife, Elaine. While I was racing in the inaugural Little 500 race back in 1988, Andy was heading over to race in Europe, where he became the first American to win the Giro d'Italia and, in doing so, also a cycling legend. Living and training in Italy, he fell in love with the dolce vita. After he retired from racing his bike, he started Cinghiale Cycling Tours to share his love of Italy's amazing riding—but also its food and drink. Whenever I can manage to be there, I help Andy and Elaine guide groups of mostly Americans through Italy's most epic regions and roads for riding.

All of this—the riding, the racing, and the passion for being on two wheels—started with the four years of competing in the Little 500 race, which cemented my love of cycling. Riding a bike just makes sense to me too. I have commuted to every job I have had. My coworkers all become used to seeing me arrive breathless, with a towel and suitable work attire in my backpack. With our planet suffocating from human choices, riding in to work is not only a pleasant wake-up but also a simple and compelling way to lessen my impact.

My teammates and I remain friends. No one strayed too far from who they were in college. Kristin did indeed go into sports management and reached the dream role of working at the Olympic Games. Not just once, but for *seven* different Olympic Games, she has traveled the world organizing every aspect of logistics just as she did for us. She has recently signed on to manage the American House for Paris 2024.

Kevin also went on to do what he had planned to do back in our college days. He became a math teacher and high school basketball coach. Unsurprisingly, he is quite a winning one at that. He recently traded out teaching high school math for elementary school physical education and loves the switch. He confided in me that while he is eligible to retire soon, he is not certain that he will as he truly enjoys his job.

Louise is also a teacher, and she's spent many years working with those learning English at various levels. She is now back in Kentucky but perfected her English language teaching over the ten years she lived in Greece. I imagine that her positivity, enthusiasm, and supportive nature make her a student favorite.

Amy continued winning bicycle races both on the road and at the Major Taylor Velodrome in subsequent years. After finishing college, she became a gym teacher. She and her military husband, Joe, did some globetrotting, stationed mostly in Germany. Her son Sam was born within a week of my own first son, Gino. Back in college, Amy and I spent a week together one summer riding across the entire state of Wisconsin on our bikes, camping out each night. Thirty years later, just as she ended her last stint living on a military base in Germany, we met up in Italy on the shores of Lake Garda near my home to reminisce, catch up on each other's lives, and of course do some pedaling together. As she headed back stateside, her choice was to live in Bloomington, where she began cycling on the same roads of our old college rides once again.

Kirsten took her ambition right into the military and climbed to the high rank of colonel by the time she retired. She was the rare woman of her generation to do so and the first in her outfit. No one who knew her in college would have doubted that Kirsten would go on pursuing firsts throughout her career. We kept in touch over the years through her occasional phone calls to the only number she had for me, that of my parents, who always enjoyed chatting with her and passed our news and constantly changing phone numbers to one another. Her "Good morning, Sunshine" rings out over the transatlantic phone calls just as emphatically now as it always did in person back in 1988.

Two years have passed now since Austin, the filmmaker, contacted me, and I now understand that all the stars must line up for a film to make it from the idea to the screen. I have learned more than I really want about all the stages from screenwriting and development to rewriting and revision to assessing competing projects to garnering a budget or studio support to understanding life rights and public domain to what might be required in selecting actors and directors. Those steps are just a beginning, and then there is an additional set of steps related to production and filming and post-production editing.

A feature film may be made from the story of the women's inaugural Little 500 race, or it may not. I have little control there. A second production company emailed me one year after Austin, saying they too wanted to make a movie about that 1988 race. Would I be willing to speak with them? I wrote back that I would but then never heard back from them—only to find that they may fictionalize the story and had already hired a screenwriter to do so. Even more recently, a third production company contacted me. Totally unrelated to the other two producers who had contacted me, this third production company offered to buy my life rights and Kirsten's as well, for a generous sum each, to tell this story. We declined unless our teammates were also included, a possibility that may still exist.

The impending film projects spurred us to reunite for the first time in years recently. We fell oddly into the same roles we had taken back on the team, Kristin and Kevin taking on the organization. We are united in wanting this story to make it to the screen but only if it is authentically portrayed, only if the film tells the real story including the Thetas' important fight for the race as well as our victory.

Given the recent interest from three different production companies, a bit surprising after the story lay dormant for thirty-five years, I realized that this story is a compelling one. I decided to sit down and tell it myself—in case the movie never makes it to the screen. You hold that work in your hands. I titled it simply *Story* for the first months I wrote it. Reflecting on the lessons that I learned in that year of my life, my freshman year of college in which I won the first women's Little 500 race with my Willkie Sprint teammates, I realized how much that year had brought me. Much of it, I had not realized during the living of the story. The recounting of that year flowed out of me and on to the glowing page on the screen of my Mac in three months' time. As it did, I played with some other titles: *Everything I Really Need to Know I Learned Riding in Little 500*. Or maybe: *Ride. Study. Love.* Or more accurately: *Eat (but no fat, sugar, or alcohol). Ride. Laugh. Love.* The story is not about winning a bike race. It is about friendship, coming of age, laughter, and love.

This is my story. Lucky me.

EPILOGUE

APRIL 29, 2023. The six members of Team Willkie Sprint were invited to be the 2023 grand marshals and guests of honor at the seventy-second running of the men's Little 500 and the thirty-fifth running of the women's Little 500. Kristin, Kevin, Kirsten, Amy, Louise, and I seized the opportunity to return to IU, excited for a homecoming to the event that had meant so much to us so many years ago. We found that Bloomington had remained charmingly frozen in time. As we kicked around campus and Kirkwood Avenue, we laughed, reminisced, and shared the happenings that had occurred in our lives over the interceding years. Coming from Italy, I brought my sixteen-year-old son, Giorgio, to see the race and the university that he had heard so much about, especially in the preceding months as I was writing this story. My sister flew in from New York, and we presented the next generation—Giorgio and her son PJ—with a valid option for college, complete with the perfect intramural sport.

I was able to meet with my English professor, Scott Sanders, now in retirement but still prolific in his writing and generous in offering to read my story. My teammates and I met with the only dorm team competing in the 2023 women's Little 500, Teter, coincidentally the team of Sanders's granddaughter Lizzie. We were given VIP treatment, as had earlier honored guests such as Lance Armstrong (before his Tour de France titles were stripped for doping violations) and President Barack Obama, who attended the women's race during his campaign. We rode in the back of the convertibles during the parade lap, something we had not done since our earlier wins, shook hands with all the athletes, and watched the races from the infield with our VIP passes. I was bestowed with perhaps the highest honor for a former rider, that of giving the starting command for the races: "Ladies/Gentleman, mount your Little 500 bicycles!"

While we noted that the Bill Armstrong Stadium had been rebuilt quite beautifully with a new press box, we were dismayed that it now had a smaller crowd capacity. Although some bleachers were erected to expand seating beyond the new sixty-five-hundred-seat capacity, no longer could the stadium hold the twenty-eight thousand fans that attended the 1988 men's race, much less the fifteen thousand that attended the inaugural women's Little 500. Kevin reasoned that this was an attempt to avoid empty stadium syndrome, while Spero Pulos—the assistant director of IUSF back in 1988 who helped bring the women's race to fruition—who had also come down for the event, thought that the reduced seating capacity may have been a deliberate attempt to quell the Little 500 weekend's out-of-control partying. I smiled at the memory. Fueled by MTV billing Little 500 as the "ultimate" college experience, the incredible influx of out-of-towners and the huge party scene during the 1988 World's Greatest College Weekend had resulted in riotous crowds quelled only by a fire truck spraying them with its hose at 4:30 a.m. Hundreds had been arrested for vandalism, disorderly conduct, and drinking violations.

We had been curious about how the racing may have evolved but were surprised to see a race that was somewhat similar to the inaugural one. The women's peloton stayed intact for a bit longer but eventually broke down. In an effort similar to our own so many years ago, the Teter team was able to break away around the halfway mark and held a quarter-lap lead for around thirty laps. That breakaway effort was quite reminiscent of the 1988 race. Eventually though, Teter was reeled in, and four teams fought it out through the last quarter of the race. Melanzana, an independent team, claimed the victory with a decisive effort in the final laps.

Twenty-seven teams partook in the women's race, up from the previous two years but lower than pre-COVID times. The race has not fully recovered from COVID-19 restrictions that canceled the 2020 races entirely and led to the running of the 2021 events in the stadium with no spectators. The women's race, which had fielded over thirty teams for each of the fifteen years previous to 2020, dipped to almost half that number in 2021 and has not yet fully recovered.

The men's race was also an exciting one, as the Cutters took their fifteenth victory in a sprint finish. My teammates and I relished watching the races and discussing strategies like the old days. Being honored as grand marshals had given a bookend to our Little 500 experience, and we loved seeing that the race meant as much as ever to the racers on the track. Most comforting was the fact that the legacy of the Kappa Alpha Thetas, Willkie Sprint, and all of the others racing with us in 1988 has been carried on, and contributed to, by riders in each successive year. Observing the young, fresh faces of the 2023 Little 500 riders, I knew that each would take something away from the race. Little 500 is about a lot more than riding bicycles around a cinder track. But their adult lives were only beginning, and they might not reflect for years on important memories or life lessons deriving from their participation in Little 500. Watching them celebrate together, I knew that friendship remained the major benefit of participating in Little 500. Their legacy, *their* Story, was no less important than my own. Who knew what this group of young women would go on to achieve? Standing on the stage issuing the starting command of the Little 500, I thought of Phyllis Klotman addressing us thirty-five years earlier and felt grateful for her support. I could not help but smile. Life had come full circle.

APPENDIX 1

1988 Little 500 Women's Race Results

Courtesy of Indiana University Student Foundation

TEAM NAME	TIME	LAPS
1. Willkie Sprint	01:10.52	100
2. Kappa Alpha Theta	01:11.01	100
3. Delta Delta Delta	01:11.19	100
4. Alpha Epsilon Phi	01:11.41	100
5. Notorious	01:11.52	100
6. Cycledelics	01:12.06	100
7. Delta Zeta	01:12.21	100
8. Stonies	01:12.22	100
9. Delta Gamma	01:12.30	100
10. Sigma Kappa	01:12.53	100
11. Collins Graitas	01:12.26	99
12. Alpha Phi	01:12.28	99
13. Kappa Delta	01:12.37	99
14. The Ambassadors	01:12.39	99
15. Cinzano	01:12.18	98
16. No Brakes-Foster	01:12.26	98
17. Alpha Xi Delta	01:12.31	98

TEAM NAME	TIME	LAPS
18. Zeta Tau Alpha	01:12.38	98
19. Alpha Omicron Pi	01:12.39	98
20. Alpha Delta Pi	01:12.47	98
21. Alpha Gamma Delta	01:12.31	98
22. Briscoe Bullets	01:12.49	98
23. Phi Mu	01:12.09	97
24. Cinquencento	01:12.21	95
25. Spokeswomen	01:12.51	93
26. Windsprint	01:12.40	93
27. Stroke Forest	01:12.41	93
28. Eureka	01:12.06	92
29. Copecetic	01:12.39	91
30. Wild Thing	01:12.35	89

1988 All-Star Rider Awards

Kerry Hellmuth	Willkie Sprint
Mia Middleton	Notorious
Jill Janov	Alpha Epsilon Pi
Martha Hinkamp	Kappa Alpha Theta
Kirsten Swanson	Willkie Sprint
Sue Hackett	Cycledelics
Suzi Bostwick	Delta Delta Delta
LeeAnn Guzek	Kappa Alpha Theta

1988 Rookie of the Year Awards

Mary Pappas	Kappa Alpha Theta
Sue Hackett	Cycledelics
Kerry Hellmuth	Willkie Sprint
Laura Mandel	Alpha Epsilon Pi

APPENDIX 2

Little 500 Women's Hall of Fame

Courtesy of Indiana University Student Foundation

The Little 500 Riders Hall of Fame is the most prestigious award given to a Little 500 rider. Each new inductee must be a graduating senior with at least three years of race experience. As the plaque reads, other criteria are as follows:

> Given to senior Little 500 riders outstanding in both ability and attitude; those who excel on the track and exemplify excellence in the Little 500; those who represent the Spirit of the Little 500 and a desire to help others.

Potential Hall of Fame inductees are nominated by a combination committee made up of Riders' Council, Steering Committee, and IUSF staff. A committee of current Hall of Fame members then meets after the race to decide who should be inducted. Their decisions then must be ratified by 50 percent of that year's Little 500 teams.

Charter Members

1988	Debbie Satterfield	STONIES
1988	Sandi Miller	ALPHA EPSILON PHI
1988	Jill Janov	ALPHA EPSILON PHI
1988	Martha Hinkamp	KAPPA ALPHA THETA
1988	Le Ann Guzek	KAPPA ALPHA THETA

Elected Members

1989	Liz Schofer	BEYOND CONTROL
1991	Kerry Hellmuth	TEAM SPRINT
1992	Kristin Youngquist	KAPPA KAPPA GAMMA
1996	Gina Murray	KAPPA KAPPA GAMMA
1996	Lisa Braun	ALPHA CHI OMEGA
1996	Greta Hoetzer	KAPPA ALPHA THETA
1997	Julie Beck	KAPPA ALPHA THETA
1998	Sara Gardner	LANDSHARKS
1999	Lindsey Hawkins	CHI OMEGA
2000	Anne Holterhoff	KAPPA ALPHA THETA
2004	Briana "Bri" Kovac	TETER WOMEN
2006	Jenn Wangerin	ROADRUNNERS
2006	Jess Sapp	KAPPA KAPPA GAMMA

APPENDIX 3

Historical Milestones Leading to a Women's Little 500 Race

Courtesy of the Indiana University Student Foundation

1973 Six women wishing to enter a team in the Little 500 were told by IUSF that women were not allowed. Although it was not specifically written into the Little 500 rules that women could not ride, IUSF was concerned about safety.

"It is true there is no reason why a woman should not ride in Little 500, but it is equally clear she would not be safe on the track," said a 1972 *Daily Student* editorial. "Given the torrid feelings of male supremacy on the track, any woman rider would be in serious trouble."

Unsatisfied with the student foundation's position, the women filed a complaint with the Bloomington Human Rights Commission (HRC). The motion was successful as the HRC issued an emergency order forcing the foundation to allow the women to ride at Qualifications. However, in the end, a legitimate rule kept the women off the track. One of their riders had transferred to IU that semester, and eligibility rules stated that transfer students could not compete. However, the barrier was finally toppled: women could no longer be kept out of the Little 500 race.

1974 A women's team filed an application but did not follow through with an attempt to qualify.

1975   One women's team registered for Qualifications but did not show up. Two other riders trained with men's teams, but neither rode in the race. One rider, Cathy Weber, broke her ankle while practicing exchanges with Rollins House, which later failed to qualify. The other, alternate Mary Brewster, quit the team that qualified nineteenth, the Cravens B team.

1976   Cathy Cerajeski became the first woman on an active team roster, with Cravens B team. However, as an alternate, she did not ride in the race. The four men who did ride finished thirty-first. Cathy later coached the 1988 Notorious team.

1977   A telephone survey conducted in the spring of 1977 by the IUSA Women's Affairs office showed that a majority of the women contacted would favor establishing a female counterpart to the Little 500 bicycle race. Of three hundred women surveyed, 54 percent indicated that they would prefer a bike race to the traditional trike race. According to Corinne Finnerty, an IUSA Women's Affairs coordinator, those favoring the replacement felt that "women [were] not presented with a serious athletic activity during Little 500. We feel this [the survey result] is an indication that something is missing in the program. We think it's important to offer women as challenging a competition as men."

1979   Women first attempted qualifying. A coed team of four women and one man competed. The team, called TBA (To Be Announced), of Leigh Parker (who lived in the Graduate Residence Center), Rhonda Pretlow (who lived in town), Robin and Laurie Calland (who lived in Willkie Quad), and Jim Studenic (also a townie) were unsuccessful in their attempt. However, they were not overly disappointed given that they were rookies and the qualifying field had included a staggering sixty-two other teams. The coaches were John Reid of men's Residence Center and Randy Bartholomew of GRC. Another team, Title IX, who also had a female rider, failed to qualify as well.

1980   Team Double Take, an all-female team, attempted to qualify for the men's race. The team was organized by sophomore Pam Swedeen. Teammates included Carol Marks (whose brother, Dean, had ridden for Lambda Chi Alpha), Cindy Alvear (IU volleyball player), and Bonnie Sullivan. The team put in a full spring of training, traveling to Florida with the Pi Kappa Phi team to train over spring break, but faltered on qualifying day. The team fouled on its first two attempts, and then on the third, they rode with extra caution to make sure each woman got one official lap for the history books. They did complete the final attempt, but their 2:54.9 time was nineteen seconds shy of the thirty-third spot.

1984   IUSF created a women's division in the Team Pursuit. Eighteen women's teams participated in this inaugural event. Finals of the Team Pursuit were held during the halftime of the IU-US Olympic Soccer Exhibition Game at Bill Armstrong Stadium. Women's winners were G.D. Zinters with a time of 11:39.13.

1985   Miss-n-Out competition was organized with both men's and women's divisions. Thirty-two women participated.

Qualifications attempt involving a woman: Sophomore Amy Kriozere and her three male teammates, the A-Team, failed to qualify with a time of 2:42.54. They missed the field by five seconds.

1987   The Stonies women's team, organized by Debbie Satterfield, won the women's division in both Miss-n-Out and Team Pursuit. In Miss-n-Out, the Stonies took the first three individual places, thus taking a dominating win in the team division over the second-place Spokeswomen and third-place Kappa Alpha Theta team.

Kappa Alpha Theta riders Lee Ann Guzek, Martha Hinkamp, Darci Feick, and Kathy Cleary attempted to qualify for the 1987 Little 500. While they were one of the top thirty-three teams at the time of their third qualification attempt, posting a time of 3:03.75, once all other teams had completed their attempts, the Kappa Alpha Theta riders had been bumped down to thirty-seventh place. Thus, another women's team fell short in an attempt to make the men's field.

Debbie Satterfield (Stonies) and Jill Janov (Spokeswomen), as veteran 1987 Little 500 Series event riders, were instrumental in gathering support across campus for a women's division of the Little 500. With help from Phyllis Klotman, dean of IU's Office of Women's Affairs, they joined IUSF officials in formulating the format for the first women's race. The only difference would be that the women would ride one hundred laps instead of two hundred and that the race would be on Friday afternoon instead of Saturday.

1988 Inaugural women's Little 500 event was held and garnered a thirty-team field. The event was won by Willkie Sprint, with over twelve thousand fans turning out to see the race. The all-freshman team riders included Kerry Hellmuth, Kirsten Swanson, Amy Tucker, and Louise Elder.

By 1988, Debbie Satterfield was a graduate student and thus did not meet eligibility rules for competing in the race she had fought so hard to establish for women at Indiana University.

2006 The first year that a full field of thirty-three teams raced in the women's Little 500. Thirty-four teams attempted to qualify, with Gamma Phi Beta losing out on the last spot in the field.

NOTES

1. Jordan Siden, "The Mini 500: The Gendered History of a Forgotten Tradition: Part 1," *Voices from the IU Bicentennial* (blog), April 17, 2017, https://blogs.iu.edu/bicentennialblogs/2017/04/17/the-mini-500-the-gendered-history-of-a-forgotten-tradition-part-1/.

2. Kat Eschner, "Although Less Deadly Than Crinolines, Bustles Were Still a Pain in the Behind," *Smithsonian Magazine*, April 21, 2017, https://www.smithsonianmag.com/smart-news/although-less-deadly-crinolines-bustles-were-still-pain-behind-180962919/#:~:text=But%20besides%20being%20deeply%20inconvenient,in%20crinoline%20fires%20in%20England.%E2%80%9D.

3. "Understanding Underwear: The Victorian Crinoline," European Fashion Heritage Association, February 14, 2020, https://fashionheritage.eu/understanding-underwear-the-crinoline/.

4. "Bloomers—Cycling—Rational Dress," Blue17, December 17, 2014, https://www.blue17.co.uk/vintage-blog/bloomers-cycling-rational-dress/.

5. These details and more on the progression of the gender equality issues related to Little 500: Jordan Siden, "The Mini 500: The Gendered History of a Forgotten Tradition: Part 3," *Voices from the IU Bicentennial* (blog), April 17, 2017, https://blogs.iu.edu/bicentennialblogs/2017/04/17/the-mini-500-the-gendered-history-of-a-forgotten-tradition-part-3/.

6. Apparently someone got this concert on film: Andy Greene, "Watch Never-Before-Seen Video of Lou Reed Jamming with John Mellencamp in 1987," *Rolling Stone*, August 12, 2020, https://www.rollingstone.com/music/music-news/watch-never-before-seen-video-of-lou-reed-jamming-john-mellencamp-in-1987-1043147/.

ACKNOWLEDGMENTS

THIS BEING MY FIRST BOOK, and one I wrote on a bit of an unexpected dare to myself, I came into the whole process blind, and I was not exactly a low-maintenance author from the vantage point of my team. I owe *mille grazie*. I thank Austin Francalancia, who saw all the elements of a tale fit for the big screen; while his film version may never come about, his spark of interest ignited my own storytelling. On a lucky day for me, Gary Dunham, the director of IU Press, picked up my online manuscript submission himself and gave me a shot. After he patiently answered roughly ten thousand questions from me, we signed a contract. Gary's patience continued—and believe me, it was tested—through the seemingly endless period finalizing my first draft. His coordination of many moving parts went far beyond any reasonable expectation and helped breathe life into this story being told. I am perennially thankful for his professionalism throughout and his significant contribution to the book you hold in your hands.

There are numerous others at IU to thank. Scott Sanders, my beloved English professor from IU, was among the first to offer to read the early drafts, and I am grateful for his encouragement and guidance. Bradley Cook, curator of photographs for IU Archives, went beyond any reasonable call of duty. He dedicated hours to combing through archived material from thirty-five years ago and managed to locate numerous photos from, no kidding, scrapbook pictures that my teammates and I had cut out of publications as obscure as IU residence hall welcome guides. I am indebted to Bradley for his methodical work and for never telling me off when yet another photo possibility surfaced. IU Archives director Dina Kellams went the extra mile by obtaining permission for me to view the WTTV4 video of the full 1988 women's race that surfaced just as I had finished the first draft. Thanks to her, I was able to test my memory and get details right. Julia Hodson at IU Studios has supported the telling of this story from the start and has lent me a hand over and over toward that end. Director Trent McGee and the IU Student Foundation helped me round out the story by generously diving into their archives to provide photos and the historical milestones for the appendix.

At IU Press, I am fairly certain that my elusive vision of the cover for this book drove David Hulsey and the design team crazy, and I am grateful for their hard work toward honoring my ambiguous requests. I greatly appreciate the improvements made by my editor, Lesley Bolton, as well as her enthusiasm about the project. My thanks to Stephen Williams, guiding me on what was needed to keep things moving in the process toward publication.

My teammates Kirsten, Amy, Louise, and Kristin; our coach Kevin; my college roommate Karen; and my best friend of many years Bob humored me when I decided on a whim to write this. It is my story but also theirs. Each would have told it differently, through their own lens. I am grateful first and foremost that they were all part of the real-life version but also for their help in adding details and corrections to the written version.

I am thankful to other friends and family members, all with busy lives, who took the time to read part or all of this story and give me feedback: Mom and Dad (somehow they're always there), Gretchan (who's been trying to coax a book out of me for years), Margie, Jennifer, Ilana, Lynn, Maria, Elaine and Oscar (whose request at ten years old that it be their next family read-aloud book humbles me), Sarah, Heyhey, Molly, PJ, and David. My son Gino was lucky to be studying in Denmark when I wrote this in a furious few months, but not his brother. Giorgio put up with hearing about all the details, having chapters read to him, listening to conversations with teammates and editors, watching me watch the race video over and over, and having his mom type away during his hockey practice from the stadium bar overlooking the ice. Early on, when he understood that I really was going to write this book, he brought me his homework luck charm—a little elephant statue that he kept nearby while writing important assignments in middle school—and placed it on my computer. Thanks, Giorgi; here's another story for you and your brother, whom I have always viewed as my own luck charms.

Kerry Hellmuth spends many of her waking hours either riding a bike or figuring out how she can fit a ride into her schedule. She is a recovering attorney and also refuses to use the PhD in behavioral economics that she worked so hard to obtain late in life at the University of Trento in Italy. She lives in Trento with her two beloved teenage sons, who remind her on a daily basis that she is old and does not know much of anything.

For Indiana University Press

Lesley Bolton *Project Manager/Editor*
Tony Brewer *Artist and Book Designer*
Brian Carroll *Rights Manager*
Gary Dunham *Acquisitions Editor and Director*
Brenna Hosman *Production Coordinator*
Katie Huggins *Production Manager*
Dan Pyle *Online Publishing Manager*
Pamela Rude *Senior Artist and Book Designer*
Stephen Williams *Marketing and Publicity Manager*